TOUR DE FARCE:
A New Series of Farce Through the Ages

THE PREGNANT PAUSE
or, LOVE'S LABOR LOST

Adaptation by Norman R. Shapiro

of

LÉONIE EST EN AVANCE
ou, LE MAL JOLI

by Georges Feydeau

(1911)

APPLAUSE
THEATRE BOOK PUBLISHERS

Library of Congress Cataloging in Publication Data

Feydeau, Georges, 1862-1921.
   The pregnant pause, or, Love's labor lost.

   (Tour de farce)
   I. Shapiro, Norman R. II. Title. III. Series.
PQ2611.E86L413   1986   842'.8   86-26586
ISBN 0–936839–58–9

APPLAUSE THEATRE BOOK PUBLISHERS
211 W. 71st Street, New York, NY 10023
(212) 595-4735

All rights reserved. Printed in the U.S.A.

First Applause Printing, 1987

Characters:

ENNEPEQUE
DE CHAMPRINET
MADAME GROSSFINGER
LEONIE
MADAME DE CHAMPRINET
ANTOINETTE

Scene:

The dining room in Hector Ennepèque's apartment. In the rear wall, left, a double door leading to the hall. To the right of the door, an electric bell. Up left, in the side wall, the door to the kitchen, opening out. In the corner, between the two doors, a low chest of drawers. Down right, the door to Léonie's bedroom, also opening out. Next to her door, against the wall, upstage, a chair. Down far right, almost on the apron, a bridge table and two chairs, left and right, facing each other. On the table, playing cards spread out in an interrupted game of solitaire. Against the rear wall, right, a sideboard. Down left, a console table, with an easy chair close by it, to the right, facing the footlights. Center, somewhat up from midstage, a round dining table set for two, with two half-eaten salads, bread, a pitcher of water, two glasses, etc. Two chairs, left and right of the table, facing each other. Overhead, a lighted chandelier. Other furniture and decorations, ad libitum.

At rise, LEONIE, *in a kimono, and* ENNEPEQUE, *in lounging pajamas and robe, are slowly walking back and forth across the stage. She is in obvious discomfort. He is encircling her waist with his left arm and holding both her hands in his. After several moments, back and forth, she stops, down right, to catch her breath.*

LEONIE: No wait... Stop... *(Groaning, as* ENNEPEQUE *obeys.)* Oh!

ENNEPEQUE *(solicitously):* Does it still hurt?

LEONIE *(bent over):* Ayyy! *(Gasping.)* Aaaah!

ENNEPEQUE: That's right... Take a deep breath... *(Illustrating.)* In... Out... In...

LEONIE *(simultaneously):* Oh, be quiet!

ENNEPEQUE: Out...

LEONIE *(groaning):* Please! Do you have to... Can't you just keep still!... Oh!

ENNEPEQUE: Sorry! I was only—

LEONIE *(suddenly):* Squeeze! Squeeze!

ENNEPEQUE: Love?

LEONIE: My hands!... Squeeze them!... Oh!

ENNEPEQUE *(complying):* Like that?

LEONIE *(grimacing):* Harder! *(Gasping.)* Squeeze them, I said... Squeeze!

ENNEPEQUE *(making an effort):* I'm trying!

LEONIE: You're not!... Harder! Harder!

ENNEPEQUE: But—

LEONIE *(still bent over, looking up at him):* Oh! If you knew what it was like...

ENNEPEQUE *(sympathetically):* I know...

LEONIE *(almost reproachfully):* You don't... You can't! You never will!

ENNEPEQUE: No... There are some things—

LEONIE *(edging toward the chair to the left of the bridge table):* Oh!... Let me sit down...

ENNEPEQUE: That's right, love... *(Helping her onto the chair.)* That's right... Here... You just relax... Nice deep breaths...

(He leaves her and goes upstage to the dining table, and sits down to continue eating his salad.)

LEONIE *(doubled over, eyes closed):* No, you can't imagine... *(She holds out her hands to where she thinks* ENNEPEQUE *is still standing.)* Here! Don't stop! Squeeze!

ENNEPEQUE *(eating):* Love?

LEONIE *(opening her eyes, with a start):* What? Where did you... *(Turning toward him.)* How can you... *(Groaning.)* Oh!... *(Holding out her hands, peremptorily.)* Squeeze them, I said! You can eat your dinner later!

ENNEPEQUE: Of course! *(Under his breath.)* What was I thinking!

(He returns and takes her hands in his. They remain for several moments facing each other without speaking, ENNEPEQUE squeezing and LEONIE voicing a variety of grunts, groans and sighs. From time to time he casts an anxious glance at his salad. Finally he begins to go through the motions mechanically, gazing off in space, resigned.)

LEONIE *(noticing his apparent attitude):* Harder! You're not squeezing!

ENNEPEQUE: Oh? Sorry!

LEONIE *(sharply):* That is, if you're sure I'm not bothering you!

ENNEPEQUE: Léonie, please...

(He keeps hold of her hands, with the result that he makes all the gestures that she makes in the following exchange.)

LEONIE *(sarcastically):* Because I'd hate to think... I am such a bother, after all!

ENNEPEQUE: Léonie...

LEONIE *(gesticulating):* I mean, I'm only the one who's got to go through all this! But it bothers monsieur!

ENNEPEQUE *(still holding her hands):* "Bothers"? When did I say—

LEONIE: Well, doesn't it? Admit it!

ENNEPEQUE: Yes! It bothers me!... Of course it bothers me to see you like this! *(Emphasizing.)* *It* bothers me... *It*... Not you...

LEONIE *(ignoring his remarks):* As if you knew what it felt like! The pain... The agony... *(With a sudden groan.)* Oh! Squeeze them! Squeeze!

ENNEPEQUE *(obeying):* Love?

LEONIE: And it's all your fault! You and your little games...

ENNEPEQUE: My little—

LEONIE: Oh, never mind! What's done is done!

(There are a few moments of silence, broken only by LEONIE's sporadic gasps, as the pain subsides.)

ENNEPEQUE: Any better?

LEONIE *(grudgingly):* A little...

ENNEPEQUE *(with a sigh of relief, letting go of her hands):* Good! I told you... Nice deep breaths...

(ANTOINETTE *enters from the kitchen, up left.)*

ANTOINETTE *(stopping at the dining table, to* ENNEPEQUE): Isn't monsieur going to eat either?

ENNEPEQUE: Later, Antoinette... Not now... Don't let it bother you...

ANTOINETTE: Bother me, monsieur? Why should it bother me? I only spent the whole afternoon—

ENNEPEQUE: I don't doubt it...

LEONIE *(still doubled up, weakly):* Antoinette...

ANTOINETTE *(up left):* Madame?

LEONIE: My mother... Has anyone let her know?

ANTOINETTE: Oh yes, madame. I telephoned Madame De Champrinet myself.

LEONIE: And the midwife?

ANTOINETTE: Yes, she must know by now. I sent the concierge... And to madame's doctor too...

LEONIE: Thank you...

ANTOINETTE: Her ostrichian...

LEONIE: My... *(Understanding.)* Yes... Thank you, Antoinette.

ANTOINETTE: Will there be anything else, madame?

LEONIE *(sighing, waving her off):* No, no... That's all...

ANTOINETTE *(removing the salad plates, grumbling under her breath):* The whole afternoon...

(She exits to the kitchen.)

LEONIE *(after a few subdued gasps, to* ENNEPEQUE*):* Oh, for heaven's sake, go eat! I can't stand that look!

ENNEPEQUE: Love?

LEONIE: I wish you could see yourself. *(She mimics his expression.)* You'd think you were some kind of martyr!

ENNEPEQUE: Me?

LEONIE: Please! Go eat your dinner! I can suffer by myself, thank you!

ENNEPEQUE: But—

LEONIE: Some of us suffer, and some of us eat. That's just the way it is. *(Waving him to the table.)* Go on! Go on!

ENNEPEQUE: But I'm not hungry! Really...

LEONIE *(pushing him away):* Please!

ENNEPEQUE *(taking a few reluctant steps toward the dining table):* Well, if you insist... But only if you're sure—

LEONIE: I'm sure!

ENNEPEQUE *(sitting to the left of the table, spreading his napkin):* Because if you need me, you know I'm right here...

LEONIE: Yes... *(With a little sneer.)* Thank you...

ENNEPEQUE *(calling):* Antoinette!

LEONIE: For all the good that does!

(ANTOINETTE appears at the kitchen door.)

ANTOINETTE *(to ENNEPEQUE):* Monsieur?

LEONIE *(continuing her lament):* This is one thing nobody can help me with.

ENNEPEQUE *(to ANTOINETTE):* You can serve me now.

ANTOINETTE: Yes, monsieur.

(She disappears, leaving the door open.)

LEONIE: It's my cross and I've got to bear it. No one can do it for me. No one, understand?

ENNEPEQUE *(who has not been paying attention):* Beg pardon?

LEONIE: No one, I said.

ENNEPEQUE *(nodding):* Aha... *(Eager to change the subject.)* Don't you think you should eat something, love?

LEONIE *(as if the idea is preposterous):* Eat?... Me? Now?

ENNEPEQUE: Just a bite?

LEONIE: Please! The very thought...

ENNEPEQUE: But just to keep your strength up...

LEONIE: Oh, don't worry about me! I'm strong... *(Turning to the cards on the table and casually continuing her solitaire.)* I'm strong...

ENNEPEQUE: Of course you are, but—

LEONIE: You have to be to go through something like this!

ENNEPEQUE *(as agreeably as possible):* I know...

LEONIE: Believe me, you have to be a tower of strength...

ENNEPEQUE: And you are... You are... Still, just a little something... Just a bite...

LEONIE *(ignoring his suggestion):* And don't you forget it! *(Proudly.)* Some day you can tell the baby what his mother went through for him! *(Tenderly, with a sigh.)* My baby...

ENNEPEQUE *(looking toward the kitchen, sniffing):* My God! I can smell it from here! What is she—

LEONIE *(appalled):* What? The baby?

(ANTOINETTE enters from the kitchen, with a plate of macaroni.)

ENNEPEQUE: No, my dinner! *(To ANTOINETTE.)* What is that, Antoinette?

ANTOINETTE *(putting it down in front of him):* Macaroni, monsieur.

ENNEPEQUE *(sniffing, with a grimace):* I see you didn't forget the garlic!

ANTOINETTE *(self-defensively)*: Oh no, monsieur! Or the pepper, either!... It's Italian. I call it "Macaroni Vesuvius."

ENNEPEQUE *(taking a taste and coughing, fanning his mouth)*: Yes! I see why!

ANTOINETTE: It takes all afternoon...

(She exits to the kitchen.)

ENNEPEQUE *(still fanning)*: Yes... Before you can feel your tongue! *(To* LEONIE.*)* Who taught that girl—

LEONIE: Please! Is that all you can think about? *(He is about to object.)* At a time like this... When you're going to become a father!

ENNEPEQUE: No... It's just that... A cook, after all...

LEONIE: If only it all comes out the way it should...

ENNEPEQUE *(misunderstanding)*: But it didn't, I'm telling you! There's much too much pepper...

LEONIE: What?

ENNEPEQUE: In her "Macaroni Vesuvius"...

LEONIE: Her... Who cares about her macaroni?

ENNEPEQUE: But you just said—

LEONIE: I said: "If only it all comes out the way it should!" I was talking about the baby...

ENNEPEQUE: Oh... I thought...

LEONIE: He's a little more important than Antoinette's macaroni! *(Pointedly.)* Or don't you think so?

ENNEPEQUE *(picking at the macaroni, ignoring her remark)* : Of course it will all come out the way it should! Why shouldn't it?

LEONIE: Because... Because I'm a month and four days early. That's why!

ENNEPEQUE: Well, what does that prove? It just shows that he's ready! He doesn't want to wait...

LEONIE: Oh yes! *(Getting up.)* It's easy for you to say! *(Dragging herself to the dining table and sitting across from him.)* I wasn't supposed to be due until next month... The twentieth... And this is only the sixteenth! *(Distraught.)* A whole month and four days!

ENNEPEQUE *(consoling her)*: Now, now, now... He's in a little hurry, that's all. He doesn't want to stay in there any longer than he has to! Can you blame him?

LEONIE: But a whole month...

ENNEPEQUE: So? He'll be a month older than other children his age. What's the harm?

LEONIE: And four days...

ENNEPEQUE: And four days...
(He picks at the macaroni again, unenthusiastically.)
LEONIE: But...
ENNEPEQUE: He'll get a good headstart!
LEONIE: But a month premature...
ENNEPEQUE: Lots of babies are premature. It happens every day. Why... Look at Julius... What's-His-Name... You know...
LEONIE: Julius? I don't know any Julius! Never in my whole life...
ENNEPEQUE: No, I mean... You know... Caesar... Julius Caesar! He was premature too. I read it somewhere... *(Embroidering the truth.)* A month and four days...
LEONIE: Oh? And where is this "Julius" person now?
ENNEPEQUE: This... Caesar? *(Chuckling.)* He's dead...
LEONIE: There! You see?
ENNEPEQUE: But he wasn't always! He used to be alive... And he lived to a ripe old age! *(Aside.)* I think...
LEONIE *(sighing):* Oh, I wish it were over! Really, I've had enough...
ENNEPEQUE *(sympathetically):* I know, love. *(Pushing away the macaroni.)* So have I!
(He picks up the pitcher and pours himself a glass of water.)
LEONIE *(with a start):* Aaah!... *(Moaning.)* Oh!...
ENNEPEQUE *(putting down the pitcher):* What's the matter?
LEONIE: They're beginning again.
(She gets up slowly.)
ENNEPEQUE: Oh my...
LEONIE *(grabbing his left hand in hers, just as he is about to pick up his glass):* Come! Walk with me!... Oh!...
ENNEPEQUE: But—
LEONIE: Never mind! You can drink later! Come! Walk with me, I said!
ENNEPEQUE *(almost resisting):* Léonie...
(As she pulls him from his seat and around the table, he reaches awkwardly for the glass with his free hand, in passing.)
LEONIE *(tugging him away):* Please! Not now, I told you!
ENNEPEQUE: Whatever you say...
LEONIE *(in pain, as they come down left):* Oh!... Squeeze!... Squeeze my hands!
ENNEPEQUE: Nice deep breaths, love... Remember...
(Once far left, they do an about-face and begin to cross right.)

LEONIE: Harder!... Harder!

ENNEPEQUE: In... Out... In... Out...

LEONIE: Harder, I said!

ENNEPEQUE: Breathe... Breathe...

(He illustrates, inhaling deeply and exhaling in her face.)

LEONIE *(stopping, turning her head with a grimace and pushing him away, but without letting go of his hands):* Pffff!... Oh, please! Don't!

ENNEPEQUE: Love?

LEONIE: Your breath... It's disgusting! All that garlic... *(With a shudder.)* Ugh!

ENNEPEQUE: All that... Oh, it's the macaroni...

LEONIE: Macaroni or not, it's... It's absolutely foul!

(They begin pacing again, back and forth.)

ENNEPEQUE *(covering his mouth with his hand and hers):* Sorry... But, "Macaroni Vesuvius," after all...

LEONIE: Really, when you see how sick I'm feeling... I should think you would have a little more consideration...

ENNEPEQUE: Considera—

LEONIE: ...and not eat macaroni and blow garlic in my face!

ENNEPEQUE *(stopping, gesturing toward the kitchen, still with her hand in his):* You tell her! She made it!

LEONIE: So? Who told you to eat it? *(In sudden pain.)* Oh!... Aaaah!

ENNEPEQUE *(at a loss):* But—

LEONIE: Squeeze!... Squeeze!

(They continue their pacing.)

ENNEPEQUE: If you let me take a drink...

LEONIE: Harder!... Squeeze harder!

ENNEPEQUE *(talking in her face):* How? How much harder... How?

LEONIE *(turning her head in disgust):* Ugh! Please! It... It... I can't stand it!

ENNEPEQUE: I'm sorry!

LEONIE: For heaven's sake, turn the other way! I can't breathe!

ENNEPEQUE *(obligingly, turning his head):* Like this?

LEONIE *(in pain, sighing):* Oh!

(They continue walking back and forth in a silence punctuated by LEONIE*'s frequent gasps and groans, with* ENNEPEQUE *straining to keep his head turned away from her face.)*

ENNEPEQUE *(after a few moments):* You know, I... I think I'm getting dizzy...

LEONIE: I don't care! Just don't breathe in my face!

ENNEPEQUE: But Léonie...

LEONIE: Squeeze harder, can't you?... Harder! They're getting worse!...

ENNEPEQUE *(resigned):* Yes, love...

(They continue pacing and squeezing.)

LEONIE: Oh!... *(Stopping, doubled up.)* Wait... I've got to stop a minute. It's too much... I've got to stop. It's killing me!

ENNEPEQUE *(still twisting his neck, with a sudden hiccup):* Hoop!

LEONIE *(misunderstanding):* Who?... Who do you think?

ENNEPEQUE: No... Hoop!

LEONIE *(impatiently):* Me, me, me! *(Pointedly.)* Not you, I'm sure!

ENNEPEQUE: No, I mean... I... Hoop!... I've got the hiccups.

LEONIE: You've got the... Isn't that nice! Monsieur's got the hiccups!... I must say, you certainly picked the right time! *(In pain.)* Oh!...

(She continues to groan and sigh from time to time throughout the following exchange.)

ENNEPEQUE: Me?... Whose fault... Don't blame me! Blame Antoi... Hoop!... Antoi... Hoop!... Antoinette and her macaroni! Is it my fault if her... Hoop!... her "Vesuvius" is erupting?

LEONIE *(imitating him):* "Nice deep breaths, love!... In, out, in, out!"

ENNEPEQUE: I can't! That's... Hoop!... That's the trouble. Every time I breathe, I... Hoop!... I hiccup!

LEONIE *(very matter-of-fact):* Then stop. They'll go away.

ENNEPEQUE: Oh yes!... Hoop!... In no time! Very nice... *(Turning toward her.)* Hoop! Hoop!

LEONIE *(pushing his head aside):* Please! I told you—

ENNEPEQUE: Sorry, I... Hoop!... I forgot... Hoop! Hoop!

LEONIE: Oh! That's enough! How many more do you have left, for heaven's sake! *(Mimicking.)* Hoop! Hoop! Hoop!... It's disgusting!

ENNEPEQUE: I'm trying... I'm... Hoop!... I'm trying...

LEONIE: Well, try harder!... Go... *(Gesturing toward the dining table.)* Take a drink! Do something!

ENNEPEQUE: With pleasure!... Hoop!... *(With a touch of sarcasm, rushing over to take his glass.)* If you're sure you... Hoop!... don't mind! I've only been trying for the last... Hoop! Hoop!... for the last—

LEONIE: Yes, yes... Stop talking and drink! My goodness!

ENNEPEQUE *(after gulping down the water)*: Hoop!... Hoop!... *(He fills the glass again and tries a variety of strategies to rid himself of the hiccups: pinching his nose and drinking, hanging his head between his knees, gargling, etc., all punctuated by an occasional "Hoop!")*

LEONIE *(while he is thus occupied)*: Of all times... Oh! This is one day I won't forget! *(She sits down to the right of the bridge table, watching ENNEPEQUE's attempts for a few moments, then looking down at her belly and addressing the unseen baby.)* I just hope you appreciate it! I hope you realize what I'm going through for you! *(With a sneer in ENNEPEQUE's direction.)* With no help from some people, thank you!

ENNEPEQUE *(apparently successful, coming down right)*: There! That's better...

(He takes a deep breath.)

LEONIE *(resting her right arm on the back of the chair, and laying her head on it, dejectedly)*: I wish I could say as much!

ENNEPEQUE *(at the bridge table, taking her left hand, sympathetically)*: Does it still hurt, love?

LEONIE *(sitting up with a sudden start, pulling her hand away, angrily)*: Of course it still hurts! *(Pounding the table with her fist.)* What kind of a question—

ENNEPEQUE *(taken aback, reacting)*: Hoop! Hoop!... Hoop! Hoop!

LEONIE *(archly)*: Again?

ENNEPEQUE: No... No... *(Taking a deep breath and holding it for several seconds, while he pinches his nose with one hand and pulls out his tongue with the other.)* There!... All gone!

LEONIE: I certainly hope so!

ENNEPEQUE *(taking her hand again, trying to be affectionate)*: Poor Léonie! I know you're not yourself!

LEONIE *(in pain)*: Oh!... Aaaah! Squeeze!... Squeeze!

ENNEPEQUE: Believe me, if I could do it for you—

LEONIE: Oh yes! Talk is cheap!... If you could do it for me...

ENNEPEQUE: But—

LEONIE *(looking down at her belly):* You've done enough already, thank you!

ENNEPEQUE: But love...

LEONIE *(suddenly struggling to her feet, in pain):* Oh!... Walk with me! Come!... Oh!...

(She pulls him violently toward her.)

ENNEPEQUE *(forced to jump over the chair to comply):* Of course!... Come!... Walk!

(They begin crossing left, to the rhythm of LEONIE*'s sighs and moans. As they reach far left and turn around to cross back, she stops short just in front of the easy chair.)*

LEONIE: No, no!... Stop! *(Pointing, weakly.)* The chair...

ENNEPEQUE: Whatever you say...

(They both sit down in the chair at the same time.)

LEONIE: Not you!... Me!... *(As he jumps up to make room for her.)* You can stand...

ENNEPEQUE: I can stand...

LEONIE *(worn out):* Oh, what torture! *(Mopping her brow.)* Look... I'm wringing wet...

(She heaves a long, desperate sigh.)

ENNEPEQUE *(after a few moments):* Any better, love?

LEONIE *(ignoring the question, in a feeble whisper):* Water... Get me a glass of water...

ENNEPEQUE *(straining to hear):* What?

LEONIE *(shouting):* Water, I said!

ENNEPEQUE: Oh... Water...

(He dashes over to the dining table.)

LEONIE: Always making me repeat...

ENNEPEQUE *(pouring some water into his glass):* But love... I couldn't hear you... *(Coming back and handing her the glass.)* There...

LEONIE *(grudgingly):* Thank you! *(Bringing it to her lips, suddenly stopping.)* Oh! Pfff!... You... This is your glass!

ENNEPEQUE: So?

LEONIE *(grimacing):* Ugh! It's all garlic...

ENNEPEQUE *(taking back the glass):* I'm sorry... The "Vesuvius"...

(He goes back to the dining table and lays it down.)

LEONIE *(shaking her head, patronizingly):* You're unbelievable! I just don't know where your head is sometimes!

ENNEPEQUE *(returning with the other glass and the pitcher):* It's just that... I've never been through this before...

LEONIE: Well? Have I?... But you don't see me going all to pieces, do you?

ENNEPEQUE *(pouring the rest of the water in the pitcher into her glass, down to the last drop, attempting a little good humor):* There! You're the old maid!

(He gives a little nervous chuckle.)

LEONIE *(taking the glass, sullenly):* Oh yes! Make jokes!... I'm in no mood for your humor!

(She gulps down the water.)

ENNEPEQUE *(solicitously):* Easy!... Not so fast... *(Taking the empty glass.)* There! Better?

(He replaces the glass and pitcher on the dining table and returns, standing behind the easy chair.)

LEONIE *(grudgingly):* A little...

ENNEPEQUE: Good! You see? I told you... Nice deep breaths...

LEONIE *(discouraged):* But not for long... I know...

ENNEPEQUE *(sympathetically):* Tsk tsk tsk!

LEONIE: You just can't imagine what it's like... The pain...

ENNEPEQUE: Tsk tsk tsk! In know...

LEONIE: You think your whole stomach is going to explode!

ENNEPEQUE *(nodding):* I know... It must be a little like my kidney stone attack.

LEONIE *(with utter disdain):* Your kidney... Don't talk to me about your... How can you compare them?

ENNEPEQUE: Well, I imagine—

LEONIE: Your kidney stone attack and... and this! That's a good one!

ENNEPEQUE *(with a nervous little laugh):* Yes... Isn't it...

LEONIE *(beginning to rage again):* It is!... It is!... It just kills you, doesn't it? To think I could possibly suffer more than you! That just kills you!

ENNEPEQUE *(protesting):* Léonie...

LEONIE: Oh no! Monsieur is the only one! No one else ever suffers! No one else knows what it's like!

ENNEPEQUE: But that's not what I—

LEONIE: No one else has the right...

ENNEPEQUE: But that's not—

LEONIE: It's my pain, and I'll thank you not to try to take it away from me!

ENNEPEQUE: But that—

LEONIE: Your kidney stone attack! Don't make me laugh!

ENNEPEQUE: But—

LEONIE: Oh! How can anyone be so... so vain!

ENNEPEQUE: Vain?

LEONIE: Vain!... *(Almost sobbing.)* Vain! Vain! Vain!

ENNEPEQUE *(resigned, nodding):* Vain...

(During the preceding exchange, ANTOINETTE *has entered from the kitchen with a platter of cheese.)*

ANTOINETTE *(crossing to the sideboard, up right, to* ENNEPEQUE): Is monsieur through with his macaroni?

ENNEPEQUE: Am I... Oh yes! Yes! Quite! *(Noticing the cheese.)* What's that?

(He gives several vigorous sniffs.)

ANTOINETTE: Some cheese, monsieur. A nice limburger...

LEONIE *(sniffing):* What? *(Categorically, to* ANTOINETTE.) Oh no! No, no, no! Not that!

ENNEPEQUE *(fanning his nose, echoing, to* ANTOINETTE): No, no...

ANTOINETTE: But monsieur... madame... It's so nice and ripe!

(She puts it down on the sideboard.)

LEONIE: Yes, I'm sure! Thank you just the same! Monsieur has put me through enough agony already... With his garlic...

ENNEPEQUE *(objecting weakly):* Oh... "Put you through..."

*(*ANTOINETTE *gives a shrug and exits to the kitchen with the rest of the macaroni, leaving the cheese on the sideboard and the other articles on the dining table.)*

LEONIE: But you don't see *me* complaining!... I don't... It's not my nature...

ENNEPEQUE *(under his breath):* Oh no! Never...

LEONIE *(overhearing, furious):* What? You're going to stand there and tell me that I do?

ENNEPEQUE *(trying to calm her down):* No, no! I didn't say that!

LEONIE: When I do all I can to keep peace... to be agreeable... And you tell me I complain!

ENNEPEQUE: I didn't... You don't...

LEONIE: A lot you know! You should see other wives! You should have one who's hard to get along with...

ENNEPEQUE: But—

LEONIE: Then you'd know!

ENNEPEQUE: You're right! You're right!... You misunderstood...

LEONIE: Me? Complain?... That's a... *(Suddenly wincing in pain.)* Oh!

ENNEPEQUE: What is it? What's the matter?

LEONIE: They're beginning again!... It's... Oh! Aaaah!...

ENNEPEQUE: See? You're getting all excited...

LEONIE *(grabbing his hands, standing up):* Come! Walk with me!... Walk...

ENNEPEQUE *(repressing an irritated sigh):* Yes, love...

(They begin crossing right.)

LEONIE: Squeeze! Squeeze!

ENNEPEQUE: I'm trying!

LEONIE *(as they reach far right, stopping):* Oh!... *(Suddenly clutching at her belly.)* Ayyyy!

ENNEPEQUE: What's the matter?

LEONIE: Oh! That one was like a knife! *(Making strained little grunts of pain.)* Ugh!... Ugh!... My God!

ENNEPEQUE: Breathe, love! Breathe!

LEONIE *(ignoring his suggestion, clutching her stomach):* Ugh!... Ugh!...

ENNEPEQUE: Try not to think of it! Think of something else!

LEONIE *(through her clenched teeth):* Ugh!... "Something else"?... Ugh! Ugh!... Like what, for heaven's sake?

ENNEPEQUE *(clenching his teeth, unconsciously duplicating her grunts):* Anything!... Anything!... Ugh! Ugh!... It's easy...

LEONIE: Oh, of course!... Ugh!... For you! You're not... Ugh!... having a baby! Ugh!

ENNEPEQUE: No... Ugh! Ugh!... You're right...

(LEONIE, doubled up, utters a crescendo of sighs, gasps and groans, which ENNEPEQUE echoes in unconscious sympathy, and during which the doorbell rings.)

LEONIE *(ending in a climactic gasp):* Aaaah!

(She takes several deep breaths as ANTOINETTE enters through the double door.)

ENNEPEQUE *(behind her):* Aaaaah!... Better?

LEONIE *(sighing):* A little...

ANTOINETTE *(to LEONIE):* Madame... It's madame... Madame's mother, madame...

LEONIE: Thank goodness!

(MADAME DE CHAMPRINET storms in behind ANTOINETTE, *and strides quickly down right, behind* LEONIE *and* ENNEPEQUE. ANTOINETTE *exits to the kitchen.)*

MADAME DE CHAMPRINET: Léonie, treasure! What's this I hear? Today?... Already?

ENNEPEQUE *(to* MADAME DE CHAMPRINET*):* Why mother... How nice—

MADAME DE CHAMPRINET *(with a sneer, as if annoyed to see him):* Yes...

LEONIE *(still clutching her stomach, without turning to look at her):* Oh, mamma! It's... It's awful! Why didn't you tell me?

MADAME DE CHAMPRINET *(sympathetically):* Precious!

LEONIE *(still without turning, holding out her left hand toward her mother, behind her):* Squeeze, mamma! Squeeze!

MADAME DE CHAMPRINET: Of course! Here, let me... *(Pushing* ENNEPEQUE *aside, impatiently.)* Out of the way!

ENNEPEQUE: Sorry...

(He goes over to the easy chair.)

MADAME DE CHAMPRINET *(taking her hand):* Don't worry! Mamma is here...

ENNEPEQUE *(sitting down, under her breath):* I can stand to sit down a minute...

MADAME DE CHAMPRINET *(continuing):* She's right here, lamb.

LEONIE: Oh!... *(Turning to* MADAME DE CHAMPRINET *.)* Walk with me!

MADAME DE CHAMPRINET: Of course, treasure!... There, there... *(They begin walking, left.)* Take nice deep breaths...

LEONIE: Yes, mamma...

MADAME DE CHAMPRINET: In... Out...

LEONIE *(trying to obey, but grunting with each breath):* Ugh!... Ugh!...

MADAME DE CHAMPRINET: There, there... I'm here... I'm here...

LEONIE *(as they approach the easy chair):* Oh, mamma! If you only knew what it's like!

MADAME DE CHAMPRINET *(with a wry little laugh):* Oh, I do! Believe me!

LEONIE *(managing a smile):* Yes, I suppose...

MADAME DE CHAMPRINET: And you weren't very easy on me, let me tell you!

LEONIE: I'm sorry! If I'd known...

MADAME DE CHAMPRINET *(smiling):* Oh, I forgive you!... And so will you, precious... When you're holding that new little De Champrinet in your arms, you'll forget...

ENNEPEQUE *(timidly, to* MADAME DE CHAMPRINET*):* Pardon me... "That little Ennepèque"...

MADAME DE CHAMPRINET *(ignoring him, to* LEONIE*):* You'll see... It's a labor of love... *(As an afterthought, realizing her* bon mot, *with a chuckle.)* So to speak!

LEONIE *(clutching at her belly):* Oh!... It couldn't have hurt this much... Years ago...

MADAME DE CHAMPRINET: Years ago... Today... What's the difference? *(Trying to be philosophical.)* Pain is pain. It doesn't improve with progress.

ENNEPEQUE *(quizzically, aside):* What?

LEONIE: Oh!...

MADAME DE CHAMPRINET *(reflecting for a moment):* I mean, it doesn't get better... I mean, worse...

LEONIE *(straining as the pain increases):* Ugh!... Ugh!...

ENNEPEQUE *(to* LEONIE*):* Breathe! Breathe!

MADAME DE CHAMPRINET *(to* ENNEPEQUE, *disdainfully):* What do *you* know? *(To* LEONIE, *embracing her.)* It's all right, treasure... It's all right. Mamma is here.

*(*ENNEPEQUE *turns aside, repressing a sigh, trying to ignore the following exchange.)*

LEONIE: Ugh!... Ugh!... *(Gasping another climactic gasp.)* Aaaaah! *(With a look of relief.)* Oh, that's better!... *(Fanning her face, sighing.)* Oh!

MADAME DE CHAMPRINET: There! You see?

LEONIE *(discouraged):* What's the good? It won't last! *(Abruptly.)* I want to sit down!

*(*MADAME DE CHAMPRINET *casts an expectant look at* ENNEPEQUE, *waiting.)*

MADAME DE CHAMPRINET *(to* ENNEPEQUE, *when he fails to react):* Well?

(She helps LEONIE *to the easy chair.)*

ENNEPEQUE: "Well"?

MADAME DE CHAMPRINET: You heard her! Get up! She wants to sit down!

ENNEPEQUE *(jumping to his feet):* Oh! Sorry... Sorry...
(He moves far left, by the console table.)

MADAME DE CHAMPRINET *(still embracing* LEONIE, *shaking her head, to* ENNEPEQUE*):* You see what your wife is going through, poor lamb! But do you lift a finger? Oh no! You just sit there and sprawl, like... like... *(Searching for an apt comparison.)* some kind of Buddha! *(To* LEONIE.*)* Sit down, precious...

*(*LEONIE *obeys.)*

ENNEPEQUE *(smiling in spite of himself):* Buddha? In an armchair?

MADAME DE CHAMPRINET: This is no time for your clever observations, monsieur!

ENNEPEQUE *(properly chastised):* No... You're right...

MADAME DE CHAMPRINET *(to* ENNEPEQUE, *pointing to* LEONIE*):* You're proud of your handiwork, aren't you?

ENNEPEQUE: Proud?

MADAME DE CHAMPRINET: Oh! It's written all over that smug face of yours!

ENNEPEQUE: I beg your—

MADAME DE CHAMPRINET: I suppose you're happy to see what you've done!

ENNEPEQUE: Happy? No!... That is, I'll be happy when it's over. Right now I'm not having much fun!

MADAME DE CHAMPRINET *(appalled at his choice of words):* Oh, really? And you think that my daughter is... *(Emphasizing.)* having fun, do you?

ENNEPEQUE: No, that's not what I—

LEONIE *(in the easy chair, clutching her stomach with both arms, to* MADAME DE CHAMPRINET*):* Don't blame him, mamma... He's not responsible...

MADAME DE CHAMPRINET *(surprised):* What? What are you saying?

ENNEPEQUE *(simultaneously):* What do you mean, I'm "not responsible"?

LEONIE *(realizing the misunderstanding):* Oh no... I mean... We didn't plan on... *(Looking down at her belly.)* on this...

ENNEPEQUE *(relieved):* Oh... Well...

LEONIE: But things like this happen. I suppose it had to, sooner or later.

MADAME DE CHAMPRINET *(to* LEONIE, *but obviously for* ENNEPEQUE): Yes! *(Counting on her fingers.)* Too bad it wasn't later!

ENNEPEQUE: But—

MADAME DE CHAMPRINET: Some people just can't control their appetite. You give them a finger and... Well, you know the rest! *(Looking squarely at* ENNEPEQUE.) A little foresight wouldn't have hurt!

ENNEPEQUE *(daring to voice a wry objection):* Excuse me, mother! I forgot to ask your permission!

MADAME DE CHAMPRINET *(taking off her coat and laying it over the chair to the right of the dining table):* My, my! More clever observations!

(She comes back down, dragging the other chair from the table.)

ENNEPEQUE: But... *(Trying to justify himself.)* You told me yourself: "I hope you're going to make me a grandmother soon!" Remember?

MADAME DE CHAMPRINET *(placing the chair beside* LEONIE): Yes, but not in seven months!

LEONIE: Eight, mamma!

ENNEPEQUE: Eight!

MADAME DE CHAMPRINET *(to* LEONIE): Yes, well... *(To* ENNEPEQUE.) Still, you should have thought twice... You didn't have to subject my daughter to... *(Pointing to* LEONIE's *sorry state.)* to...

ENNEPEQUE: Believe me, if there had been some other way...

MADAME DE CHAMPRINET *(sitting on the chair, to* LEONIE): Poor lamb!

LEONIE: Don't pity me, mamma. *(Stoically.)* We all go through it.

MADAME DE CHAMPRINET: There's my brave little girl! Just like your mother, precious... Suffering in silence!

ENNEPEQUE *(jaw dropping, about to object, but resisting):* Ah...

(The doorbell rings.)

MADAME DE CHAMPRINET *(to* LEONIE): Ah! I hope that's your father.

LEONIE: Oh no, mamma! You didn't tell papa, I hope!

MADAME DE CHAMPRINET: Of course I did, treasure. I sent word to his club.

LEONIE: Oh my! I wish you hadn't! I wanted to spare him until it was over. No need to upset him...

MADAME DE CHAMPRINET: Why not? He deserves his little share, like the rest of us.

LEONIE: Poor papa!

MADAME DE CHAMPRINET: "Poor papa"? "Poor..." What about "poor mamma"? Don't I count? Or are men the only ones that matter?

LEONIE: No... It's just that—

MADAME DE CHAMPRINET *(with a glance toward* ENNEPEQUE*):* Men!... Always men!... That's why they're such heartless, inconsiderate beasts!

ENNEPEQUE *(under his breath):* Much obliged!

LEONIE *(to* MADAME DE CHAMPRINET*):* But... *(Sweetly.)* Papa's not a man!

MADAME DE CHAMPRINET: Well, maybe not to you...

LEONIE *(suddenly clutching her stomach again):* Oh!...

MADAME DE CHAMPRINET: What's the matter, precious? Are they starting again? *(*LEONIE *nods.)* Do you want to walk?

*(*LEONIE *nods again.)*

ENNEPEQUE *(rushing over to* LEONIE*):* Yes... Come...

MADAME DE CHAMPRINET *(stopping him in his tracks):* Not with you!

ENNEPEQUE: But I... But—

MADAME DE CHAMPRINET *(losing patience):* Oh!... Go boil some water! *(To* LEONIE, *about to help her up.)* Come, treasure...

LEONIE: Never mind. I don't have to. That was only a small one.

*(*ANTOINETTE *enters from the hall and comes down toward the easy chair.)*

ANTOINETTE *(to* LEONIE*):* It's the delivery man from the store, madame. With the things...

LEONIE: Yes... Monsieur will be right there.

ENNEPEQUE *(to* LEONIE*):* Things? *(To* ANTOINETTE.*)* What things?

ANTOINETTE: A basset...

ENNEPEQUE: What?

LEONIE *(correcting):* A bassinette...

ANTOINETTE: Yes... And baby clothes... And three dozen diapers...

ENNEPEQUE: Three dozen—

ANTOINETTE: For Monsieur Jean-Jacques, monsieur.

MADAME DE CHAMPRINET *(surprised):* Jean-Jacques?

LEONIE *(to* ANTOINETTE*):* Monsieur will help you.

ANTOINETTE: Yes, madame.

(She is about to leave.)

LEONIE *(stopping her):* Is everything else ready in his room, Antoinette?

ANTOINETTE: Yes, madame.

LEONIE: Good! And you won't forget to put a rattle in his crib...

ANTOINETTE: No, madame.

(She exits to the hall.)

LEONIE *(to* ENNEPEQUE, *who is lingering):* Well?

ENNEPEQUE: Yes, love... Right away...

(He follows ANTOINETTE *out the door.)*

MADAME DE CHAMPRINET: So... Jean-Jacques... *(Rather amused.)* It's going to be a boy, I see!

LEONIE *(confidently):* Oh yes, mamma!

MADAME DE CHAMPRINET: It's definite. You're sure...

LEONIE: Absolutely! It couldn't be anything else. We decided...

MADAME DE CHAMPRINET *(nodding):* Of course!... And if it happens to be a girl? I mean, if it just happens... You're going to put it back, I suppose?

LEONIE *(rather testily):* But I'm telling you, it's a boy! *(Offering proof.)* Why, I hardly had any morning sickness at all in the beginning. And... And I don't show a bit in the front. That proves it...

MADAME DE CHAMPRINET *(smiling):* Yes, I'm sure!

LEONIE: Besides, there's the moon...

MADAME DE CHAMPRINET: Oh?

LEONIE: Everyone knows that when a baby is conceived at a full moon, it's a boy. But when the moon is—

MADAME DE CHAMPRINET *(laughing):* Please! No astronomy lessons! I take your word! *(Dragging the chair back to the dining table.)* Monsieur Jean-Jacques it is!... *(With a smile, moving right.)* Until further notice!

(ENNEPEQUE enters from the hall, followed by ANTOINETTE. She is carrying the bassinette, piled high with a variety of baby

clothes and diapers. At the bottom of the pile, unseen, is a child's chamber pot.)

ENNEPEQUE *(coming center with* ANTOINETTE*)*: Here it is... Everything he needs!

*(*ANTOINETTE *lays the bassinette down on the dining table as* LEONIE *gets up and, painfully, goes to join them.)*

LEONIE *(as enthusiastically as her condition permits)*: Oh look! All his little things!... *(Picking articles out and holding them up to* MADAME DE CHAMPRINET.*)* His little shoes!... His diapers!...

ENNEPEQUE *(moving down right, under his breath)*: Three dozen!

LEONIE *(clutching at her belly)*: Oh!...

(She reaches for the chair to the left of the table.)

MADAME DE CHAMPRINET *(helping her sit down)*: Try not to think of it! Think of something else!

LEONIE *(docilely)*: Yes, mamma... I'm trying... *(Picking more articles out of the bassinette.)* His little blouse!... His little nighty!... *(To* ANTOINETTE.*)* Thank you, Antoinette... You can put it all in his room.

MADAME DE CHAMPRINET *(to* ANTOINETTE, *pointedly)*: Monsieur Jean-Jacques's room!

ANTOINETTE *(to* LEONIE*)*: Yes, madame.

(She turns to leave, but before she takes a step LEONIE *spies the chamber pot at the bottom.)*

LEONIE *(taking it out)*: Oh look! His little potty!

MADAME DE CHAMPRINET: Isn't that darling!

LEONIE *(holding it up, emotionally)*: His own personal little potty! *(As* ANTOINETTE *exits to the hall.)* Just think! In a couple of years... *(Lyrically, giving it a little kiss.)* My little Jean-Jacques...

(During the preceding, MADAME DE CHAMPRINET, *without taking her eyes off her daughter, has come down right, between* LEONIE *and* ENNEPEQUE.*)*

MADAME DE CHAMPRINET *(emotionally, to* ENNEPEQUE*)*: Just like me when I was expecting!

ENNEPEQUE *(uninterested)*: Oh?

MADAME DE CHAMPRINET *(pointing to* LEONIE, *dotingly)*: I loved her even before she was born!

ENNEPEQUE: Yes... *(Aside.)* I waited a little longer...

LEONIE *(holding the pot toward* ENNEPEQUE*)*: Here! Look at it...

(She passes it to MADAME DE CHAMPRINET. *The latter passes it in turn to* ENNEPEQUE, *then sits down at the bridge table.)*

ENNEPEQUE: Yes... I see...

(He looks around, not quite sure what to do with it.)

LEONIE *(watching him handle it with utter indifference):* Doesn't that do anything to you?

ENNEPEQUE: Doesn't what...?

LEONIE: His potty...

ENNEPEQUE *(without much conviction):* Oh yes!... Yes...

LEONIE *(with a note of pride):* Not as much as it does to me!

ENNEPEQUE *(sensing an impending disagreement):* Of course it does, love! *(*LEONIE *watches him pass the pot from hand to hand, and she begins to chuckle quietly.)* What's so funny?

LEONIE: Nothing... I just can't help thinking...

MADAME DE CHAMPRINET: Precious?

LEONIE *(to* MADAME DE CHAMPRINET, *still laughing):* Nothing...

ENNEPEQUE: What?

LEONIE *(to* ENNEPEQUE, *laughing harder):* Nothing...

ENNEPEQUE *(almost jovially, pleased at the change of tone):* But it must be something! Tell us!

MADAME DE CHAMPRINET *(to* LEONIE, *smiling):* Tell us, treasure...

LEONIE: No!... *(Relenting.)* It's just that... *(To* ENNEPEQUE.*)* When I saw you standing there with his potty, I remembered a silly dream I had last night.

ENNEPEQUE *(smiling):* About a chamber pot?

LEONIE *(still laughing):* Yes! Isn't that absurd?

MADAME DE CHAMPRINET *(categorically):* It's good luck!

LEONIE: Imagine... The two of us were at the races... *(To* ENNEPEQUE.*)* You and I... I was dressed in my fancy grey gown, and you were in your morning-coat. But instead of your top hat, you were wearing... *(She laughs.)* You were wearing a chamber pot!

*(*ENNEPEQUE *suddenly stops smiling.)*

ENNEPEQUE: I what?

MADAME DE CHAMPRINET: What a charming idea!

ENNEPEQUE: It's stupid, if you ask me!

(He moves left, by the console table, annoyed.)

LEONIE: And you were so proud! You stood there tipping it to everyone you saw! I was mortified!

MADAME DE CHAMPRINET *(laughing):* I imagine!

LEONIE: And I kept telling you: "Hector! Hector, please!..." *(Slowly and emphatically.)* "Take it off! They're all staring!" But all you could say was: "No, no! I think it's fetching! I'm starting a new style!"

ENNEPEQUE: You and your dreams!

LEONIE *(to* MADAME DE CHAMPRINET*):* I wish you could have seen him, mamma!

MADAME DE CHAMPRINET *(still laughing):* Funny!...

LEONIE: "Funny" isn't the word!

MADAME DE CHAMPRINET: I'm sure!

(They continue laughing for a few moments at ENNEPEQUE's *expense. He is obviously not amused.)*

LEONIE *(to* MADAME DE CHAMPRINET*):* And you know... Actually it didn't look bad on him at all! It really was rather... fetching!

ENNEPEQUE *(aside):* I'll bet.

LEONIE *(to* ENNEPEQUE, *casually):* Show her... Put it on your head and let her see how you looked.

ENNEPEQUE *(turning toward her, aghast):* Put it—

LEONIE *(never doubting his compliance, to* MADAME DE CHAMPRINET*):* You'll see...

ENNEPEQUE: I beg your... Not in a million years!

LEONIE *(to* ENNEPEQUE*):* What?

ENNEPEQUE: Of all the silly—

LEONIE *(offended):* You won't do a simple little thing when I ask you?

ENNEPEQUE: Why me?

LEONIE *(pointing to* MADAME DE CHAMPRINET*):* Just for her! For mamma! So she can see—

ENNEPEQUE: I don't care! Not even for the Pope!

MADAME DE CHAMPRINET *(shaking her head):* Tsk tsk tsk!

ENNEPEQUE *(to* LEONIE*):* What do you take me for? A chamber pot on my head! Are you out of your mind?

LEONIE: But it's new. It's never been used.

ENNEPEQUE: I don't care! New or used, it's still a chamber pot!

MADAME DE CHAMPRINET *(getting up and taking a few steps left, to* ENNEPEQUE*):* What's the harm? No one will know.

ENNEPEQUE: I will! That's enough!

LEONIE *(getting up, joining* MADAME DE CHAMPRINET*)*: See? He won't do a little thing like that to make me happy!

ENNEPEQUE: Léonie... Really...

MADAME DE CHAMPRINET *(to* ENNEPEQUE*)*: I could understand if she asked you to wear it in public. At the races... Or at your club... But here...

ENNEPEQUE: Not here, not anywhere! Nowhere! I'm sorry!

LEONIE *(petulantly)*: But I want you to! I want you to put it on!... I want to see it!

ENNEPEQUE: And I don't want to!... And you won't!... And that's that!

LEONIE *(stamping her foot)*: I want you to! I want you to!

ENNEPEQUE: No! No! No!

MADAME DE CHAMPRINET *(butting in, to* ENNEPEQUE*)*: Monsieur... Hector... Please!

LEONIE *(continuing)*: I want you to! I want you to!

MADAME DE CHAMPRINET *(embracing* LEONIE, *to* ENNEPEQUE*)*: You can't refuse a pregnant woman! It's dangerous!

ENNEPEQUE: Bah!

MADAME DE CHAMPRINET: Who knows what could happen to the baby...

LEONIE: I want you to!

MADAME DE CHAMPRINET: ...to Jean-Jacques!

ENNEPEQUE: No! I'm sorry!

LEONIE *(to* MADAME DE CHAMPRINET*)*: See? What kind of a father...

MADAME DE CHAMPRINET *(approaching* ENNEPEQUE, *left)*: Please! Be reasonable!

ENNEPEQUE: I won't!

LEONIE *(to* ENNEPEQUE*)*: You will! You will!

ENNEPEQUE *(to* LEONIE*)*: I won't! And that's final!

LEONIE: Oh!... What does he care what happens to his son?... Or to me!

ENNEPEQUE: Léonie...

LEONIE *(clutching at her belly, with a huge groan)*: Ohhhh!... Aaaay!

MADAME DE CHAMPRINET: Precious? *(To* ENNEPEQUE.*)* There! Now you've done it! You see?

LEONIE *(doubling up)*: Ugh!... Ugh!...

MADAME DE CHAMPRINET *(guiding her to the chair to the right of the bridge table, to* ENNEPEQUE, *sharply)*: Put it on!

LEONIE *(falling in a heap on the chair, turning away from* ENNEPEQUE*):* He doesn't care...

ENNEPEQUE *(holding out the pot, to* MADAME DE CHAMPRINET*):* Here! You put it on, why don't you!

LEONIE: He doesn't...

MADAME DE CHAMPRINET *(moving left, to* ENNEPEQUE*):* Believe me, if she asked me to...

LEONIE *(head in hands, almost sobbing):* Heartless beast!

ENNEPEQUE *(to* MADAME DE CHAMPRINET*):* Well, I'm asking you! What's the difference? *(Imitating.)* "Put it on! Put it on!"

MADAME DE CHAMPRINET: Don't be foolish! You're not pregnant!

LEONIE *(with subdued gasps and groans):* Oh!... Ugh!... Aaaay!

MADAME DE CHAMPRINET *(to* LEONIE*):* Poor lamb! *(To* ENNEPEQUE.*)* Can't you see what you're doing?

ENNEPEQUE *(beginning to weaken):* But...

MADAME DE CHAMPRINET: Please! For your wife!... For your son!...

ENNEPEQUE *(with less and less conviction):* A grown man, for goodness' sake... I'm thirty-eight years old, and you're asking me to—

MADAME DE CHAMPRINET: So? What of it? *(Wheedling.)* Be a dear!... *(Almost humbly.)* Please, Hector!... Put it on!

ENNEPEQUE *(about to give in):* But...

LEONIE *(weakly):* Ugh!... Ugh!...

ENNEPEQUE *(aside):* Why couldn't she just want a sour pickle or something?

MADAME DE CHAMPRINET *(to* ENNEPEQUE*):* Go ahead...

ENNEPEQUE *(resisting):* Besides, it's not my size... It's too small...

MADAME DE CHAMPRINET: How do you know? You haven't tried it.

ENNEPEQUE: I can tell. It won't fit.

MADAME DE CHAMPRINET *(coaxing):* Try! Let's see!

ENNEPEQUE *(with a sigh of resignation, about to comply):* Oh... *(Stopping, in a final moment of revolt.)* No! I'm sorry!

LEONIE *(still facing right, her head still in her hands):* Ugh!... Oh!...

*(*ENNEPEQUE *hesitates, lifts the pot to his head, stops, hesitates again a few times, and finally acquiesces.)*

ENNEPEQUE *(putting it on, furiously):* All right! *(To* LEONIE.*)* I hope you're happy! *(To* MADAME DE CHAMPRINET.*)* Both of you!

MADAME DE CHAMPRINET *(joining* LEONIE, *down right, pointing):* There, precious! You see? He did it! He put it on!

*(*LEONIE *turns her head to look.)*

ENNEPEQUE *(crossing right, squatting in front of the bridge table to give* LEONIE *the full effect, still fuming):* Yes! *(Pointing.)* You see? Look! You see?

(The doorbell rings.)

LEONIE *(looking at him for a moment):* Oh, my God! Don't you look stupid!

ENNEPEQUE *(flabbergasted):* What?

LEONIE: I've never seen anything so ridiculous! *(Waving him off.)* Get away!

ENNEPEQUE: What did you—

LEONIE: Get away! I can't look at you!

ENNEPEQUE *(turning to* MADAME DE CHAMPRINET*):* Did you hear—

MADAME DE CHAMPRINET *(coming down to* ENNEPEQUE, *pulling him away, up left):* Never mind! Just don't upset her!

(She returns down right to LEONIE, *still sitting at the bridge table.)*

ENNEPEQUE *(behind the easy chair, exasperated):* Oh!...

*(*ANTOINETTE *enters from the hall, and without noticing* ENNEPEQUE, *crosses down right to the two women.)*

ANTOINETTE *(to* MADAME DE CHAMPRINET*):* Madame... *(To* LEONIE.*)* Madame... It's Madame What's-Her-Name... The midwipe... *(She mispronounces.)*

ENNEPEQUE *(furious, to* ANTOINETTE*):* Tell her to go to blazes!

LEONIE and MADAME DE CHAMPRINET *(together):* What?

*(*ANTOINETTE *turns at the sound of* ENNEPEQUE*'s voice and finds herself face to face with him.)*

ANTOINETTE *(noticing the pot on his head, with a start):* Oh! Monsieur must be crazy!

ENNEPEQUE *(misinterpreting her observation, repeating):* I said: "Tell her to go to blazes!"

MADAME DE CHAMPRINET *(to* ANTOINETTE, *calmly):* Show her in, Antoinette.

ANTOINETTE. Yes, madame.

(She turns to leave.)

ENNEPEQUE: What? *(To* ANTOINETTE, *who is almost at the hall door.)* Antoinette, I said...

*(*ANTOINETTE *stops and looks at him.)*

ANTOINETTE: Yes, monsieur. I know...

(She shakes her head, shrugs, and exits.)

ENNEPEQUE *(grumbling to himself):* What do they think I am? Do this... Do that... *(Lifting the pot up off his head with both hands, imitating* LEONIE.*)* "Put it on! I want to see!... Put it on! Put it on!..." *(He replaces it squarely on his head.)* And when I do... *(Coming down right, standing in front of* LEONIE.*)* When I stand there like a jackass... *(He hits the bridge table with his hand.)* Does she thank me?

LEONIE *(with a grimace of disgust):* Take it off! I can't stand to look...

MADAME DE CHAMPRINET *(to* LEONIE*):* He will, treasure...

ENNEPEQUE *(hands on hips, categorically, to* MADAME DE CHAMPRINET*):* Oh no he won't! *(To* LEONIE.*)* It's staying right where it is!... You wanted it... *(Giving the pot a sharp little tap.)* You've got it! Look to your heart's content!

MADAME DE CHAMPRINET *(conciliatory):* Hector...

ENNEPEQUE *(ignoring her, to* LEONIE*):* I'm tired of doing somersaults every time you crack the whip... Every time you get a new bee in your bonnet!

LEONIE: What?

ENNEPEQUE *(looking at* MADAME DE CHAMPRINET*):* Both of you!

(He begins pacing left and right, as MADAME GROSSFINGER, *a severe, ample-bosomed amazon, enters from the hall, in coat, hat and gloves. She is followed by* ANTOINETTE, *who is carrying her overnight bag.* LEONIE, *with* MADAME DE CHAMPRINET's *help, rises slowly to greet her.)*

MADAME GROSSFINGER *(striding down right, nodding, to* LEONIE, *with a German accent):* Madame... *(To* MADAME DE CHAMPRINET.*)* Madame...

*(*LEONIE *returns her nod and sits down again at the bridge table, this time on the chair to the left, as* ANTOINETTE *places the bag on the floor to the right of the easy chair, and exits to the hall.)*

MADAME DE CHAMPRINET *(nodding):* Madame... *(Correcting.)* Frau Grossfinger...

MADAME GROSSFINGER *(turning to* ENNEPEQUE *just as he is about to pass behind her):* Monsieur... *(Taken aback at the sight of the chamber pot.)* My, my!

ENNEPEQUE *(with a quick little tip of the pot, in greeting):* Madame...

MADAME GROSSFINGER *(pointing to the pot):* Your head, monsieur... It's cold, maybe?

ENNEPEQUE *(as offhand as his anger will allow):* Oh no... It's just that pregnant women make such curious requests! *(Looking squarely at* MADAME DE CHAMPRINET.*)* And you mustn't refuse them!

MADAME GROSSFINGER *(to* MADAME DE CHAMPRINET*):* What? You...?

MADAME DE CHAMPRINET: No, no... *(Pointing to* LEONIE.*)* My daug·.ter...

MADAME GROSSFINGER: Aha...

ENNEPEQUE *(taking off the pot, holding it against his body with his forearm, like a top hat, to* MADAME GROSSFINGER*):* You see... *(Sarcastically.)* It's a symbol, madame!

MADAME GROSSFINGER: It is?

ENNEPEQUE: Of a man who jumps when his wife snaps her fingers!

MADAME GROSSFINGER: So?... Why not? *(*ENNEPEQUE *gives a little sigh of disgust.)* Please... For me, you don't shtand on ceremony! Keep it on... I don't mind...

ENNEPEQUE *(to himself):* Of course... On, off... Off, on...
(He places the pot, angrily, on the floor by the console table, and sits down in the easy chair.)

MADAME GROSSFINGER *(to* LEONIE*):* Und this is our new young mamma-to-be, ja?

LEONIE: Yes, madame...

MADAME DE CHAMPRINET *(behind* LEONIE*):* And soon, if you ask me. The pains are closer and closer.

MADAME GROSSFINGER: Fine!... Fine!... *(To* LEONIE.*)* The sooner the better, ja?

LEONIE: Oh, yes!

MADAME GROSSFINGER: We don't want to keep it waiting...

LEONIE *(correcting):* "Him," madame!

MADAME GROSSFINGER: Him, her, it... Whatever... *(Taking off her gloves.)* In the profession we say: "When it knocks, go open the door!"

MADAME DE CHAMPRINET *(nodding):* Yes... Quite...

MADAME GROSSFINGER *(to* MADAME DE CHAMPRINET*):* Just between you und me, I didn't expect so soon... *(To* LEONIE.*)* Next month your obstetrician said, ja?

LEONIE *(embarrassed):* I... I thought so, but...

MADAME GROSSFINGER: But?

LEONIE: It must be premature...

MADAME GROSSFINGER: Und you're sure... No mistake... No flaw in your calculations...

LEONIE: Oh no! There can't be. I've hardly been married eight months...

MADAME DE CHAMPRINET *(to* MADAME GROSSFINGER, *reiterating):* That's right... Eight months...

MADAME GROSSFINGER: Aha... Und... *(With a meaningful wink and a wag of the finger.)* Not before?

LEONIE: Oh, madame!

MADAME DE CHAMPRINET *(simultaneously):* Certainly not!

MADAME GROSSFINGER *(to* MADAME DE CHAMPRINET*):* No, no... I'm only asking for professional reasons. *(To* LEONIE.*)* I have to know what to expect.

LEONIE: Of course... *(Suddenly wincing in pain again.)* Oh!... Aaaay! *(Clutching her stomach.)* Oh my!...

MADAME DE CHAMPRINET: Precious?

LEONIE: That was the worse one yet...

(She doubles up in pain.)

MADAME GROSSFINGER: So! That's fine!

LEONIE *(objecting):* Fine? What's fine about it?

MADAME GROSSFINGER: It means that our little visitor is getting ready...

MADAME DE CHAMPRINET *(nodding):* To knock!

MADAME GROSSFINGER: Ja!

LEONIE *(to* MADAME GROSSFINGER, *testily):* Ugh!... That's easy for you to say! It's not your door he's knocking on!

MADAME GROSSFINGER: Oh, I know, madame! Believe me... Two times I went through it...

MADAME DE CHAMPRINET *(pretending to be interested):* Oh?

MADAME GROSSFINGER *(to* MADAME DE CHAMPRINET*):* Und each one... A good ten pounds! If you think that was a circus...

MADAME DE CHAMPRINET: Tsk tsk tsk!

MADAME GROSSFINGER: Of course, mine weren't... *(To* LEONIE.*)* as you say... premature...

LEONIE *(groaning, to* MADAME GROSSFINGER*)*: How much longer...?

MADAME DE CHAMPRINET*(to* MADAME GROSSFINGER*)*: Yes... When will she deliver?

MADAME GROSSFINGER *(to* LEONIE*)*: It's hard to tell exactly until I examine you. *(To* MADAME DE CHAMPRINET.*)* I don't diagnose *in vacuo,* madame. *(She pronounces "wacuo.")*

MADAME DE CHAMPRINET: Where?

MADAME GROSSFINGER: "Where"?

MADAME DE CHAMPRINET: In... You said, "in..."

MADAME GROSSFINGER: *Vacuo... In vacuo...* That's Latin...

MADAME DE CHAMPRINET *(feigning comprehension)*: Yes... Of course...

MADAME GROSSFINGER *(to* LEONIE*)*: But better, I think, you get ready, ja...

LEONIE *(still in obvious pain)*: Yes... I think so... *(Wincing.)* I'm sure!

MADAME GROSSFINGER: Let mamma tuck you in... I come see you bye und bye.

(She takes off her coat.)

LEONIE *(standing up)*: Yes... Right away...

MADAME DE CHAMPRINET *(helping her)*: Come, precious... Come... *(To* MADAME GROSSFINGER, *nodding.)* Madame...

(She helps LEONIE *out the door, down right, as they both exit.* MADAME GROSSFINGER, *coat under her arm but still wearing her hat, surveys the room, completely ignoring* ENNEPEQUE. *Her eye lights on the electric bell next to the hall door. As* ENNE-PEQUE, *watching her, gets up and stands by the easy chair, she goes upstage, rings the bell, then comes back down to the easy chair to retrieve her overnight bag.)*

MADAME GROSSFINGER *(finding* ENNEPEQUE *standing in front of the bag, peremptorily)*: Out of my way!

ENNEPEQUE *(stepping aside)*: Oh...

(She puts her coat and gloves on the back of the chair, picks up the bag and opens it. As she takes out a long white smock, a white apron, and an instrument case, laying them on the seat of the chair, ANTOINETTE *enters from the kitchen.)*

ANTOINETTE *(to* ENNEPEQUE*)*: Monsieur rang?

ENNEPEQUE: No!... It was madame...

ANTOINETTE *(looking around the room, obviously expecting to find* LEONIE*)*: Oh? Where is she?

ENNEPEQUE *(pointing to* MADAME GROSSFINGER*):* This madame...

MADAME GROSSFINGER *(arranging the articles on the chair):* Ja, mademoiselle... You're boiling?

ANTOINETTE: Madame?

MADAME GROSSFINGER: The water... You're boiling?

ANTOINETTE: Oh yes, madame. *(Pointing to the kitchen.)* Lots...

MADAME GROSSFINGER: Und plenty towels?

ANTOINETTE: Well... Will diapers do?

ENNEPEQUE *(under his breath):* We only have three dozen!

MADAME GROSSFINGER *(to* ANTOINETTE*):* I suppose... Und cotton? Und alcohol? Und—

ANTOINETTE: Oh yes, madame. Everything the doctor said to get.

MADAME GROSSFINGER: So! Go bring...

ANTOINETTE: Yes, madame.

(She exits to the kitchen.)

MADAME GROSSFINGER *(turning aside, with the empty bag in her hand, and bumping into* ENNEPEQUE*):* Out of my way!

ENNEPEQUE *(moving aside):* Sorry...

MADAME GROSSFINGER *(putting the bag on the chair to the left of the bridge table, thinking that* ANTOINETTE *is still behind her, gesturing down left to the console table):* Und you put everything on that table, ja?

ENNEPEQUE: I do?

MADAME GROSSFINGER: What?

ENNEPEQUE: You said—

MADAME GROSSFINGER: Not you! *(Looking around.)* Where's the maid?

ENNEPEQUE: She left.

MADAME GROSSFINGER: So... I tell her when she comes back. *(About to move left, but blocked by* ENNEPEQUE*.)* Out of my way!

ENNEPEQUE *(moving aside, annoyed):* Of course...

(MADAME GROSSFINGER goes over to the console table and spreads out a large white cloth. ENNEPEQUE, curiously, gradually approaches and stands behind her, peering over her shoulder.)

MADAME GROSSFINGER *(turning around, bumping into him):* Again?

ENNEPEQUE: Sorry...

MADAME GROSSFINGER: Who are you, monsieur? What do you do here?

(She takes the instrument case from the easy chair.)

ENNEPEQUE: Do? *(Almost apologetically.)* I... I'm the husband...

MADAME GROSSFINGER *(spreading the instruments out on the console table):* You're the... Ah... Ja, you must be... *(Pointing to his head.)* The chamber pot... Ja... *(Nodding.)* Ja, you must be...

ENNEPEQUE: Yes... *(Mumbling.)* I must be... *(He watches her work for a few moments in silence; then, in an effort to be as agreeable as possible.)* My, my! That looks complicated! *(She ignores him.)* All those things... It must take a lot of training to learn how to use them! *(Still no reaction from her.)* It's not easy being a midwife, I'll bet!... *(He clears his throat a few times as she continues to ignore his observations.)* I suppose you keep busy... With all your experience... *(Asking a question, point blank, to elicit some reaction.)* Do you make many deliveries a year, madame?

MADAME GROSSFINGER *(finally turning around, impatiently):* "Make," monsieur? I don't "make" deliveries! *(Attempting humor.)* I'm not the shtork!

(Finished at the console table, she goes over to the easy chair.)

ENNEPEQUE *(following her):* No... "Do," I mean... How many do you do?

MADAME GROSSFINGER *(finally taking off her hat, curtly):* Quite a few!

ENNEPEQUE *(pretending to be interested):* Aha... And when you do them, do you—

MADAME GROSSFINGER *(cutting him off, sharply):* Please, monsieur! Your wife is having a baby! I don't have time to teach you my profession!

ENNEPEQUE: No... No...

MADAME GROSSFINGER *(holding out her hat, along with her coat and gloves from the chair):* Here! Go hang somewhere...

ENNEPEQUE *(taken aback):* What?

MADAME GROSSFINGER *(shoving them into his hands):* Ja! Run along now! I'm busy...

ENNEPEQUE *(objecting weakly):* I... I beg your—

MADAME GROSSFINGER *(waving him off):* Run along! Run along!

ENNEPEQUE: Of all the... Oh!

(He exits to the hall, mumbling and grumbling. MADAME GROSSFINGER *moves left, unbuttoning her blouse. As she takes it off and lays it on the back of the easy chair, the kitchen door opens and* ANTOINETTE *appears, carrying a tray with the diapers and a variety of medicinal accessories: packages of cotton wadding, several bottles and flasks, etc.)*

MADAME GROSSFINGER *(jumping at the noise, modestly clutching her arms to her bosom):* Who's there?

ANTOINETTE: It's only me, madame. I'm back with the things...

MADAME GROSSFINGER *(relieved):* Ah!... So!... *(Taking her smock from the easy chair and pointing to the console table.)* Over there...

ANTOINETTE: Yes, madame.

(She comes down left and arranges the articles next to the instruments already laid out, while MADAME GROSSFINGER *gets ready to slip into her smock. Just then the hall door opens and* ENNEPEQUE *enters.)*

ENNEPEQUE *(coming around the dining table and down right):* There! All put away!

MADAME GROSSFINGER *(at the easy chair, with a start):* Don't come in! Don't—

*(*ANTOINETTE *rushes over to help shield her.)*

ENNEPEQUE *(noticing her state of undress, turning aside):* Oh, sorry... I didn't realize...

MADAME GROSSFINGER *(hurrying to put on the smock, with* ANTOINETTE's *help):* You couldn't knock, for heaven's sake?

ENNEPEQUE: To come into my own dining room?... *(With a shrug.)* I never do...

MADAME GROSSFINGER *(furious):* I don't care what room!... My shoulders und my bosom were exposed, monsieur! *(Facing him and pulling open the front of her smock to prove her point.)* See?

ENNEPEQUE *(nodding, as casually as possible, while she takes her apron from the easy chair):* Aha...

MADAME GROSSFINGER *(putting on the apron, turning, and bumping into* ENNEPEQUE, *who has followed behind her):* Oh!... Shtill?

ENNEPEQUE: Beg pardon!

MADAME GROSSFINGER: You don't have something to do?... Some place to go?

ENNEPEQUE: To go? Me?

MADAME GROSSFINGER: I couldn't work mit people breathing down my neck! *(Picking up her blouse from the easy chair.)* Please! A little consideration, ja?

ENNEPEQUE *(retreating right, by the bridge table):* Oh?

(MADAME GROSSFINGER, blouse in hand, moves right, ostensibly to get the empty bag lying on the chair to the left of the bridge table.)

MADAME GROSSFINGER *(finding her way blocked by* ENNE-PEQUE, *losing patience):* Out of my way!

ENNEPEQUE: Sorry...

(He moves left, around her.)

MADAME GROSSFINGER *(stuffing the blouse into the open bag and holding the latter out to* ENNEPEQUE*):* Here!... Mit my coat!

ENNEPEQUE *(taking the bag and holding it out to* ANTOINETTE, *who has returned to the console table):* Antoinette!

MADAME GROSSFINGER: No, no! Not "Antoinette!" If I mean "Antoinette" I say "Antoinette!"... I need her here to help...

ENNEPEQUE *(with a sigh):* I see...

MADAME GROSSFINGER *(waving him off):* So go... Run along...

ENNEPEQUE *(resigned, mumbling):* "Run along..." *(Turning to leave, aside.)* Attila the Hun! *(Mimicking, under his breath.)* "Run along! Run along!"

(He exits through the hall door.)

MADAME GROSSFINGER *(putting on the apron):* So! *(To* ANTOINETTE.*)* Now we get to work!

ANTOINETTE: Yes, madame.

MADAME GROSSFINGER: First, you go make sure the water is boiling, ja? Und when it is...

ANTOINETTE: I make the coffee!

MADAME GROSSFINGER *(with a wry smile):* No.

ANTOINETTE: The camomile?

MADAME GROSSFINGER: When it is, you bring in a big basin... To madame's room...

ANTOINETTE *(as she finishes arranging the articles on the console table):* Oh...

(A knock is heard at the hall door.)

MADAME GROSSFINGER *(still down right):* Come in!

(ENNEPEQUE enters, and comes down to the easy chair.)

ENNEPEQUE *(with a little bow, to* MADAME GROSSFINGER*):* You see? I knocked.

MADAME GROSSFINGER: Ja, ja!... What's the good? Now I'm not naked!

ENNEPEQUE: Well, how could I tell? I don't peek through keyholes.

MADAME GROSSFINGER *(with a note of doubt):* Oh?

ENNEPEQUE *(with affected deference):* Will there be anything else, madame? Any other little errands?

MADAME GROSSFINGER *(on whom the sarcasm is lost):* No, no... *(Waving him off.)* Out of my way!...

(She crosses left, in front of him.)

ANTOINETTE *(to* MADAME GROSSFINGER*):* And me, madame?

MADAME GROSSFINGER: No, no... You do what I told you, ja? *(To* ENNEPEQUE, *abruptly.)* Und what time is dinner?

ENNEPEQUE: Dinner? We've had it.

MADAME GROSSFINGER: Who? Not me!

ENNEPEQUE: Tsk tsk tsk!

MADAME GROSSFINGER: I was sitting down, just, when your concierge came und told me.

ENNEPEQUE *(repeating, more emphatically):* Tsk! Tsk! Tsk!

MADAME GROSSFINGER: You mean... Nothing?

ENNEPEQUE *(with the memory of the macaroni still fresh in his mind):* That depends... How hungry are you?

MADAME GROSSFINGER: What difference? I don't eat because I'm hungry. I eat because it's time. *(Looking at her watch.)* Und my time is now...

ENNEPEQUE: Well... *(With an inquisitive glance at* ANTOI-NETTE.*)* I'm sure Antoinette can scrape up something.

ANTOINETTE: Yes, monsieur.

MADAME GROSSFINGER *(to* ANTOINETTE*):* So!... Und what was the soup?

ANTOINETTE: Madame?

MADAME GROSSFINGER: What kind did you have?

ANTOINETTE: We didn't...

MADAME GROSSFINGER *(disappointed):* No soup?

ENNEPEQUE: We never have it.

MADAME GROSSFINGER *(to* ENNEPEQUE*):* But I do!

ENNEPEQUE *(nodding):* Aha...

MADAME GROSSFINGER: All the time!

ENNEPEQUE: Well...

MADAME GROSSFINGER: Oh, ja, ja! I know... Today it's out of shtyle... Soup? Ha!... Old-fashioned!... So! Me too!... *(Disdainfully.)* That's progress!... You could keep it!

ENNEPEQUE: Yes...

MADAME GROSSFINGER: Who knows where it's going to take us?... *(In the same tone of voice.)* Und what's next?

ENNEPEQUE *(misinterpreting her question, trying to be agreeable):* Who knows? Maybe nothing at all!

MADAME GROSSFINGER *(surprised):* You mean, no soup... Und then, nothing?

ENNEPEQUE *(realizing that he has misunderstood):* Soup?... Oh, no... I—

MADAME GROSSFINGER: Nothing?

ENNEPEQUE: Excuse me... I thought you meant... That is... You said: "Progress... What's next?..." And I thought you meant—

MADAME GROSSFINGER *(impatiently):* No, no!... After the soup!

ENNEPEQUE: Aha!... Well... After the soup... the soup we didn't have... we had a small salad, and then macaroni.

ANTOINETTE *(interjecting, proudly):* Vesuvius!

MADAME GROSSFINGER *(to ANTOINETTE):* What?

ENNEPEQUE *(to MADAME GROSSFINGER, with an intent evidently lost on ANTOINETTE):* Antoinette's delicious "Macaroni Vesuvius"... *(Aside.)* Molten lava flambé!

ANTOINETTE *(to ENNEPEQUE):* Thank you, monsieur.

ENNEPEQUE: With a subtle hint of garlic and a *soupçon* of pepper...

MADAME GROSSFINGER *(with a nod of approval, to ENNEPEQUE):* Ja... Und then?

ENNEPEQUE: Then?

MADAME GROSSFINGER: After that?

ENNEPEQUE: That was all.

MADAME GROSSFINGER *(with a gesture of disappointment):* Pfff! That's not so much...

ANTOINETTE *(to ENNEPEQUE):* Monsieur forgot the limburger.

ENNEPEQUE: Yes, so I did. *(Turning toward the sideboard, under his breath.)* But the memory lingers on.

MADAME GROSSFINGER *(to ENNEPEQUE):* Shtill... What kind of a meal... *(As ANTOINETTE goes over to the dining table to remove* MADAME DE CHAMPRINET's *coat from the chair on the right.)* A bird would eat more!

ENNEPEQUE: You might say...

MADAME GROSSFINGER *(going up to the dining table):* So... *(To* ANTOINETTE.*)* You bring your "Vesuvius" what's left, und a nice salad.

(She sits down on the right.)

ANTOINETTE *(behind the table, carefully folding* MADAME DE CHAMPRINET's *coat):* And what would madame like to drink? White wine or red?

MADAME GROSSFINGER: No, no...

*(*ENNEPEQUE, *in front of the table heaves a premature sigh, aside.)*

ANTOINETTE: No?

MADAME GROSSFINGER: No... Champagne only...

ENNEPEQUE: Champagne?

MADAME GROSSFINGER: Ja! Better for my liver...

ANTOINETTE *(to* ENNEPEQUE*):* And it goes very well with my "Vesuvius," monsieur!

ENNEPEQUE: Oh, I'm sure!... *(To* MADAME GROSSFINGER.*)* Do you drink it all the time?

MADAME GROSSFINGER: Ja, ja! *(Hinting.)* When my patients send me a case or two...

ENNEPEQUE: Yes... Well... *(Going up to* ANTOINETTE, *who has moved up left, between the dining table and the hall door, in a whisper.)* Look... Run downstairs, Chez Pierre, and get the cheapest bottle he has...

ANTOINETTE *(to* ENNEPEQUE, *aloud, naively):* Why, monsieur? *(Pointing to the kitchen.)* We still have that bottle from monsieur and madame's wedding...

ENNEPEQUE *(trying unsuccessfully to silence her):* Shhh!

ANTOINETTE *(not to be deterred):* The expensive one... The one monsieur was saving...

ENNEPEQUE: Shhh!

ANTOINETTE: The "Veuve Click-Clock"...

MADAME GROSSFINGER *(pricking up her ears):* Cliquot? Veuve Cliquot? *(To* ANTOINETTE.*)* Ja, that would do fine... *(*ENNEPEQUE *comes down left, with a frustrated sigh.)* Not the best... But Veuve Cliquot would do... Ja!... *(To* ANTOINETTE.*)* Und just one bottle... More than one I never drink...

ANTOINETTE: Very good, madame. And when would madame like me to serve?

MADAME GROSSFINGER (*getting up and coming downstage*): Any time... When it's ready...

ANTOINETTE: About ten minutes then...

MADAME GROSSFINGER: Fine! (*Looking toward* LEONIE's *room.*) Time we have plenty.

ENNEPEQUE (*to* MADAME GROSSFINGER, *crossing right*): We do?

MADAME GROSSFINGER: Oh, ja! (*Very professionally.*) When the mother-to-be is a *primipara,* it takes longer.

ENNEPEQUE: A what?

MADAME GROSSFINGER: A *primipara*...
(*She sits down to the left of the bridge table as* ANTOINETTE *clears away what is left on the dining table, except for a few crusts of bread.*)

ANTOINETTE (*to* MADAME GROSSFINGER): Oh, she's not, madame!

MADAME GROSSFINGER (*surprised*): She's not?

ANTOINETTE (*naively*): No! She's a De Champrinet... I mean... (*Glancing at* ENNEPEQUE.) She was...

MADAME GROSSFINGER: No, no!... *Primipara*... That's Latin...

ANTOINETTE: Oh...
(*She exits, with a shrug, to the kitchen.*)

MADAME GROSSFINGER (*to* ENNEPEQUE): You know... Like *vivipara*...

ENNEPEQUE (*pretending*): Of course...

MADAME GROSSFINGER (*with a show of erudition*): From *vivi*... (*She pronounces "weewee."*) Und *para*... When the baby comes out whole...

ENNEPEQUE (*aside*): I should hope so!

MADAME GROSSFINGER: Und not an *ovipara*... From *ovum,* egg...

ENNEPEQUE (*nodding*): Yes... Yes...

MADAME GROSSFINGER: So... She is a *primipara,* ja? I mean, only eight months... Und this is her first marriage?

ENNEPEQUE (*completely at sea*): Why yes...

MADAME GROSSFINGER: Then I assume... No, she wouldn't be a *multipara*... (*Reflecting.*) Unless, of course... (*Wagging her finger.)* Before... *(Shaking her head.)* Mit so much progress, who could be sure!

ENNEPEQUE *(still befuddled):* Yes... You're so right...

MADAME GROSSFINGER: But *you* must know, monsieur! She never told you?

ENNEPEQUE: Oh... Dozens of times!

MADAME GROSSFINGER: So? Tell me, ja?... *Primipara* or *multipara?* Which is she?

ENNEPEQUE *(hesitating):* Oh... *(Finally, taking the plunge, categorically.)* Multipara... Yes, if you really have to know...

MADAME GROSSFINGER *(taken aback):* She is?... Tsk tsk tsk! Young people today!... Such a nice little thing, too!... Oh well, at least that makes it easier... Und faster, ja! Better I get busy!

(She crosses briskly left, to the console table.)

ENNEPEQUE *(nodding, as if understanding):* Yes... Please...

MADAME GROSSFINGER *(puttering with her instruments, turning to him):* Und how many did she have mit the other... Or others...?

ENNEPEQUE: "How many?"

MADAME GROSSFINGER: Babies! How many babies?

ENNEPEQUE: Madame Ennepèque?... What babies? This is her first!

MADAME GROSSFINGER *(confused):* But you said... Then she is a *primipara*...

ENNEPEQUE: She is?

MADAME GROSSFINGER: If this is her first!

ENNEPEQUE: Yes! What made you think—

MADAME GROSSFINGER: But just now you said... When I asked you...

ENNEPEQUE: Sorry... *(Sheepishly.)* I must have misunderstood the question...

MADAME GROSSFINGER: Well... *Primipara*... *Multipara*... *(Crossing right, toward* LEONIE'*s room.)* It's time, I think, we pay our patient a visit!

ENNEPEQUE *(following on her heels):* Yes... Let's—

MADAME GROSSFINGER *(turning around so quickly that* ENNE-PEQUE *bumps into her):* Not you!... I don't work mit an audience! I told you...

ENNEPEQUE: But... Her husband...

MADAME GROSSFINGER *(adamantly):* Husbands, lovers... I don't care! No shpectators!

ENNEPEQUE *(outraged):* Lovers?... My wife has no lovers!

MADAME GROSSFINGER: I don't care! No shpectators!... Nobody! Period!

(She does a brisk about-face at the threshold.)

ENNEPEQUE *(objecting):* But...

MADAME GROSSFINGER *(turning to him with a withering glance, and pointing to the ground, as if commanding a dog):* Shtay!... Shtay!...

(She exits to LEONIE's *room and closes the door behind her.)*

ENNEPEQUE *(on whom the intent has not been lost):* Of course!... Woof woof! Woof woof! *(Speaking at the door, to the unseen* MADAME GROSSFINGER, *angrily.)* I can do tricks too! *(He sits up and begs like a dog.)* Woof woof!

*(*ANTOINETTE *enters from the kitchen carrying a basin of water. She notices* ENNEPEQUE *barking at the door, and almost drops the basin.)*

ANTOINETTE *(catching it in time):* Monsieur! What on earth—

ENNEPEQUE *(turning to her, angrily):* Nothing! Don't ask!

ANTOINETTE: Oh... *(Crossing down right.)* I though maybe monsieur was having an attack of nerves... What with madame and all—

ENNEPEQUE: Forget it, I said! It's nothing!... You didn't see it!

(The doorbell rings.)

ANTOINETTE *(hesitating between the water and the bell):* Monsieur... I wonder if...

ENNEPEQUE *(still very much on edge):* What? What is it?

ANTOINETTE: The door... Could monsieur please answer it? I'm busy with madame...

ENNEPEQUE: Where the devil is Etienne?

ANTOINETTE: He's out, monsieur.

ENNEPEQUE: Very nice!

ANTOINETTE *(at* LEONIE's *door):* And I've got to bring this...

(The bell rings again.)

ENNEPEQUE: Don't bother! She won't let anybody in! Not even me!

ANTOINETTE: But I have to, monsieur... *(The bell rings again.)* Please... *(With a nod toward the door, holding up the basin.)* If monsieur would just knock... I can't...

ENNEPEQUE: I'm telling you, you're wasting your time!

(He knocks.)

MADAME GROSSFINGER's VOICE: You can't come in!

ENNEPEQUE *(to* ANTOINETTE*):* See?
(The bell rings again, longer.)

ANTOINETTE *(shouting through the door):* It's me, madame...
Antoinette...

MADAME GROSSFINGER's VOICE: Oh, ja!... I thought...
(Opening the door, to ANTOINETTE.*)* Come in!

*(*ANTOINETTE *gives* ENNEPEQUE *a little curtsy, enters, and
closes the door. The bell rings again, still longer.)*

ENNEPEQUE *(looking at the closed door, hands on hips):*
Damnation!... Now isn't that nice! *(There are several more repeated
rings.)* Yes, yes!... I'm coming!... Of all the times...

*(He exits to the hall, grumbling under his breath, leaving the
door open. The stage is empty for several moments, during the
following exchange offstage.)*

DE CHAMPRINET's VOICE: I must say, you took your time!

ENNEPEQUE's VOICE: I'm sorry, but Etienne is out and everyone
was busy...

(DE CHAMPRINET *appears at the hall door, in evening dress,
with his coat over his arm, wearing his top hat and carrying his
cane.)*

DE CHAMPRINET *(entering):* Really, she couldn't have chosen a
more inappropriate moment! *(To* ENNEPEQUE, *entering behind
him.)* Or you either, monsieur!

(He comes down, far right.)

ENNEPEQUE *(hanging back a little):* Well, we didn't exactly plan
it...

DE CHAMPRINET: No, I'm sure you didn't! If you had... My
word, you'd have given us a little more notice, for one thing!

ENNEPEQUE *(rather deferentially):* But it's hardly my fault...

DE CHAMPRINET *(facing him squarely):* Well I'd like to know
whose then! *(Tipping his hat, with a little nod.)* It's certainly not
mine!

ENNEPEQUE: I didn't mean—

DE CHAMPRINET: There I was at my club, waiting for dinner,
playing a spirited game of casino... With the duke... As usual...

ENNEPEQUE *(under his breath):* Of course...

DE CHAMPRINET: A hundred francs a hand... And winning, I'll
have you know!... Well, just as I was sitting with a handful of
points, all of a sudden, out of a clear blue sky, I got the news.
"Lovely!" I thought. "They have to pick a time like this..."

ENNEPEQUE: But—

DE CHAMPRINET *(ignoring him, continuing):* Still, despite the inconvenience, a father has his duty...

ENNEPEQUE: I'm sorry!

DE CHAMPRINET *(sitting down to the right of the bridge table):* Even when he's holding a hand like mine... *(Taking off his hat and laying it on the table.)* So I put down my cards and I said to the duke: "Cher ami, you must excuse me. Another De Champrinet is about to sally forth..."

ENNEPEQUE *(timidly):* Excuse me... *(Sitting down across from him.)* An Ennepèque...

DE CHAMPRINET *(still ignoring him):* ...and continue my line...

ENNEPEQUE: And mine...

DE CHAMPRINET: ...of illustrious forebears!

ENNEPEQUE *(with a shrug):* Well...

DE CHAMPRINET: He applauded!

ENNEPEQUE: How thoughtful!

DE CHAMPRINET *(standing up, putting on his hat):* He was delighted to see me get up and leave... and take my luck with me! *(Moving toward LEONIE's door.)* Now then, is she in here?

ENNEPEQUE: Yes, but you can't go in. The midwife is with her. She'll bite your head off...

DE CHAMPRINET: What?... *(Grumbling.)* My own daughter... *(Taking off his hat and putting it, with his coat and cane, on the chair to the right of the dining table.)* Then at least you can let me have something to eat... After making me miss dinner!

(He moves left, still grumbling.)

ENNEPEQUE *(still seated):* Well, if you don't mind leftovers... There's not very much...

DE CHAMPRINET: What choice do I have? Besides, I'm not hungry... With all the excitement...

(ANTOINETTE enters from LEONIE's room.)

ENNEPEQUE *(stopping her):* Ah! Antoinette!... Set a place for Monsieur De Champrinet. He's eating too.

ANTOINETTE: Yes, monsieur.

ENNEPEQUE *(pointing):* And please take his hat on the way out.

ANTOINETTE: Yes, monsieur.

(She picks up the coat, hat and cane from the chair, and exits to the hall.)

DE CHAMPRINET: "Too"?... Who else? Do you have guests?

ENNEPEQUE: Only one.

DE CHAMPRINET: Oh?

ENNEPEQUE: The midwife.

DE CHAMPRINET *(annoyed):* You mean... I'm dining with the midwife?

ENNEPEQUE: Well...

DE CHAMPRINET: "Well" indeed!

ENNEPEQUE: Just today... Under the circumstances...

DE CHAMPRINET *(behind the bridge table):* Hmm! I suppose there's no harm... Just this once... *(Looking down his nose.)* But, a midwife... *(Sitting down again, across from him, shaking his head.)* What in heaven's name got into her, to have the child today? I thought it was next month...

ENNEPEQUE: Yes... *(Sheepishly.)* I guess she's ahead of schedule.

DE CHAMPRINET: You guess!... Lovely! *(Picking up the cards and shuffling them mechanically as he speaks.)* He guesses she's ahead of schedule! Not even eight months... What on earth will people think?

ENNEPEQUE *(offhand):* Well...

DE CHAMPRINET: "Well" indeed! Don't tell me "well"! I know what they'll think! And so do you, monsieur! *(Not giving* ENNE-PEQUE *time to object.)* They'll think you decided to have an appetizer before the entrée!

ENNEPEQUE: Monsieur!

DE CHAMPRINET: That's what they'll think! And I can't say I blame them!

ENNEPEQUE: But—

DE CHAMPRINET *(still mechanically shuffling):* The duke, the marquis, the baron... And their wives, good God! I can just hear them now! "So, that's why De Champrinet gave his daughter to that commoner!"

ENNEPEQUE: Oh!

DE CHAMPRINET *(continuing):* "He had to! Yes, he had to!..." Lovely!

ENNEPEQUE: But monsieur! It's not true!

DE CHAMPRINET: True or not, that's what they'll say! *(Handing him the deck to cut.)* Here... Every last one of them! You'll see!

ENNEPEQUE *(trying to defend himself):* But... Eight months... One month premature... *(Cutting the cards.)* It happens every day!

DE CHAMPRINET: Of course! Every day!... *(Dealing out the cards for a game of casino: four apiece and four face up on the table.)* But not to a De Champrinet, my friend! At least, it's not supposed to... *(Picking up his hand.)* You go first...

ENNEPEQUE *(picking up his hand):* Well... *(DE CHAMPRINET opens his mouth to reply.)* I know...

DE CHAMPRINET: "Well" indeed!

ENNEPEQUE *(simultaneously):* "Well" indeed!

(They proceed to play during the following dialogue.)

ENNEPEQUE: If you're going to worry about the least little thing! Like what your friends think!... *(He throws down a card.)* Two of spades...

DE CHAMPRINET: "Least little thing!" That's a good one! *(Taking the card with one of his.)* I'll take it... Certainly I'm going to worry! *(ENNEPEQUE throws down another card, which DE CHAMPRINET also picks up with one of his.)* My word, she's my daughter!

ENNEPEQUE *(laying a card on a face-up card):* Building fives...

DE CHAMPRINET: *My* daughter, monsieur! *(Taking the trick.)* My trick...

ENNEPEQUE: I know, but still... *(Throwing down a card.)* Five...

DE CHAMPRINET *(taking the card):* Mine... It's a question of honor... You wouldn't understand...

ENNEPEQUE *(as* DE CHAMPRINET *deals four more cards apiece):* Oh? Thank you, I'm sure... *(Throwing down a card.)* Ten... You seem to be forgetting, monsieur, she's my wife!

DE CHAMPRINET: It's not the same!... *(Taking the card.)* Ten of diamonds... My lucky day... Blood, monsieur... Blood...

ENNEPEQUE *(laying a card on another one):* Building nine... What about it?

DE CHAMPRINET *(taking the trick):* It's thicker than water!

ENNEPEQUE *(throwing down a card):* Water?... I hardly think...

DE CHAMPRINET *(taking his card):* No, it's just not the same...

ENNEPEQUE: Maybe not, but... *(Laying a card on another.)* Building eight... And with a spade... If everyone worried about what everyone said...

DE CHAMPRINET: Not everyone, monsieur!... *(Taking his trick.)* Eight? Thank you... They can gossip all they like about anyone else...

(He deals again.)

ENNEPEQUE *(playing):* King of clubs...

DE CHAMPRINET *(throwing down a card):* It's my family I'm concerned with!

ENNEPEQUE: I know, but if they're wrong... *(Playing.)* Building kings...

DE CHAMPRINET: Wrong? *(Taking the trick.)* Thank you... Try to prove it! Just try!

ENNEPEQUE *(playing):* Four of spades... I should think...

DE CHAMPRINET *(playing):* Building five, with an ace... There are some things people are too ready to believe!

ENNEPEQUE: Yes, but still... *(Throwing down a card.)* I should think...

DE CHAMPRINET *(taking his trick):* It's too late now! You should have thought before!

(He deals again.)

ENNEPEQUE: Monsieur?

DE CHAMPRINET: It's too late to think now... *(ENNEPEQUE plays a card.)* The horse is out of the stable... *(Under his breath, taking the card.)* Or almost...

ENNEPEQUE: Really... How many times do I have to tell you... *(They play quickly through the deck, occasionally announcing their tricks and punctuating their play with appropriate exclamations. It is clear that DE CHAMPRINET is winning.)*

DE CHAMPRINET *(as they reach the end of the deal, returning to his idée fixe, shaking his head):* Eight... Eight...

ENNEPEQUE *(playing his last card):* Seven!

DE CHAMPRINET *(throwing down his last card, misunderstanding):* Seven?... Good heavens, don't make it worse!

ENNEPEQUE: What?

DE CHAMPRINET: Eight months is bad enough!

ENNEPEQUE: No, I mean... *(Pointing.)* My card...

DE CHAMPRINET: Your... Oh! You can have it!... *(Tallying up his points as ENNEPEQUE picks up the remaining cards and counts.)* Cards... Spades... Ten of diamonds... Deuce... Aces... *(To ENNEPEQUE.)* Clean sweep! You owe me a hundred francs.

ENNEPEQUE *(agape, about to throw down his cards, holding them in the air):* I... A hundred... What are you talking about? *(Throwing them down.)* We weren't playing for—

DE CHAMPRINET: "Weren't playing..." Then what the devil were we doing?

ENNEPEQUE: We were playing... Playing...

DE CHAMPRINET: Well?

ENNEPEQUE *(pointedly):* "Well" indeed!... But not for money! Not for a hundred francs!

DE CHAMPRINET: Then why didn't you say so before we began?

ENNEPEQUE *(flustered):* Why... I...

DE CHAMPRINET: Not now, after I win!

ENNEPEQUE: You... You didn't ask! Why should I—

DE CHAMPRINET: But I always play casino for a hundred francs a hand! I just told you, not five minutes ago! Remember?

ENNEPEQUE: Yes, but... You... Not me...

DE CHAMPRINET: My word, what kind of rules do you play by? If you win, I pay... If I win, you don't!

ENNEPEQUE: But—

DE CHAMPRINET: Really, is that fair?

ENNEPEQUE: I'm sorry, monsieur! Not one franc! It's the principle...

DE CHAMPRINET *(getting up, moving upstage):* Some people!... See if I ever play with you again, my friend!

ENNEPEQUE *(glancing toward* LEONIE's *room):* Believe me, if you think I feel like playing cards...

DE CHAMPRINET: And you think I do?... It's habit, that's all... *(Gesturing toward the door.)* With my daughter in there... Going through who knows what!

ENNEPEQUE *(getting up):* And all this time!

(He goes over to the door.)

DE CHAMPRINET *(joining him):* Poor child!

ENNEPEQUE: What's taking so long?

(They both bend over and listen at the keyhole.)

DE CHAMPRINET: Shhh! Maybe I can hear—

(Just at that moment, the door is suddenly pulled open and MADAME GROSSFINGER *appears, backing out with a basin full of water. As she turns, downstage she bumps into* ENNEPEQUE, *splashing him, but missing* DE CHAMPRINET, *who backs away in time.)*

ENNEPEQUE: Oh!

MADAME GROSSFINGER *(to* ENNEPEQUE*):* You again? *(Down center.)* Very nice!

ENNEPEQUE: "Very..." Look what you've done!

MADAME GROSSFINGER: Maybe that would teach you to shtay out of my way...

ENNEPEQUE *(down far right):* Look! I'm drenched!

MADAME GROSSFINGER: ...und not to go peeking through keyholes, ja!

ENNEPEQUE: "Peeking through—"

MADAME GROSSFINGER *(looking squarely at* DE CHAMPRINET): Und you too!

DE CHAMPRINET: What?

MADAME GROSSFINGER *(to* DE CHAMPRINET): At your age! Tsk tsk tsk!

ENNEPEQUE *(to* MADAME GROSSFINGER): Madame, I assure you, I don't...

DE CHAMPRINET *(to* ENNEPEQUE): What did she say?

ENNEPEQUE *(moving center, under his breath)*: Keyholes!... *(To* MADAME GROSSFINGER.*)* Of all the... Thanks to you I've got to go change! Very nice!

MADAME GROSSFINGER: So! *(Holding out the basin.)* Here!... In the kitchen!...

(She thrusts it into his hands.)

ENNEPEQUE: Me?

MADAME GROSSFINGER *(waving him off)*: Run along! Run along!

ENNEPEQUE *(furious, striding up left)*: Oh!... *(Under his breath.)* Damn pain in the... *(Stopping at the kitchen door, glaring at her.)* Woof woof! Woof woof!

(He turns and exits, slamming the door.)

DE CHAMPRINET *(to* MADAME GROSSFINGER): What was that?

MADAME GROSSFINGER: I couldn't imagine!

(She sits down in the easy chair.)

DE CHAMPRINET *(after a pause)*: Well now, how's everything going?

MADAME GROSSFINGER *(looking him up and down, archly)*: You mind your own business!

DE CHAMPRINET *(appalled)*: What?

MADAME GROSSFINGER: My personal life I don't discuss mit shtrangers!

DE CHAMPRINET: Your personal... No, no!... I mean... *(At* LEONIE's *door, pointing.)* In there!... When can I go in?

MADAME GROSSFINGER: You couldn't! No meddlers, thank you!

DE CHAMPRINET *(outraged)*: "Peddlers..." I'm not a—

MADAME GROSSFINGER *(correcting)*: Meddlers... Meddlers...

DE CHAMPRINET: "Meddlers"? I'm her father!

MADAME GROSSFINGER: Oh? Maybe so... But to a midwife, monsieur, you're just another meddler. We couldn't have it!

DE CHAMPRINET *(calming down):* Well...

MADAME GROSSFINGER: You give her a kiss when she delivers, not before! Und then, just in und out...

DE CHAMPRINET *(acquiescing):* I see... I see... And is Madame De Champrinet with her?

MADAME GROSSFINGER: Your shpouse?

DE CHAMPRINET: My... Yes, is she in there?

MADAME GROSSFINGER: I should hope so, ja!

DE CHAMPRINET: And she's not just another meddler?

MADAME GROSSFINGER *(standing up):* She's a mother, monsieur. That's different.

DE CHAMPRINET: Aha... Well, if it's not too much trouble, please tell her I'm here.

MADAME GROSSFINGER: Ja! I tell her... If she cares!... *(Moving toward* LEONIE's *door, waving him away.)* Now out of my way!

DE CHAMPRINET *(stopping her at the door):* I must say, madame... You're not an easy woman to get along with!

MADAME GROSSFINGER *(not understanding):* Please?

DE CHAMPRINET: I said: "You're not an easy woman—"

MADAME GROSSFINGER *(hands on hips):* I should hope not, monsieur! I'm not one of your floozies!

DE CHAMPRINET: My—

MADAME GROSSFINGER: I'm too old to carry on mit every gigolo I meet!

DE CHAMPRINET *(realizing the source of her confusion):* Excuse me, but I wasn't exactly suggesting... *(With a chuckle.)* "Carry on" indeed!

MADAME GROSSFINGER *(mellowing):* Of course, that wouldn't mean I don't have my moments...

DE CHAMPRINET: Oh?

MADAME GROSSFINGER *(quoting):* "A little nonsense now und then..."

DE CHAMPRINET: "Is relished by the wisest men!" *(Nodding.)* I know... Very true...

MADAME GROSSFINGER *(at* LEONIE's *door, about to enter):* But not during business hours, monsieur!

DE CHAMPRINET: No... Certainly not!... *(With a little mock salute.)* Well, madame... Carry on!

MADAME GROSSFINGER *(turning):* Are you making fun?

DE CHAMPRINET *(realizing what he has said, with a little laugh):* No, no... That just slipped out.

MADAME GROSSFINGER: Ja! I'm sure!

(She exits.)

DE CHAMPRINET *(sitting down to the left of the bridge table, sighing):* My, my, my, my, my, my! *(Picking up the cards and shuffling.)* "Not one of your floozies!" *(Laughing.)* No, I daresay!... *(Mechanically dealing out a hand of casino to himself and an imaginary opponent.)* Mine or anyone else's, madame!... Not likely!... *(He puts down the pack and looks at his hand.)* Ah! The ace of spades!... *(Laying it down on one of the four cards face up on the table.)* Building ten... *(He pauses for a moment, then looks at the opponent's hand.)* Hmm! He's got the ten of diamonds!... *(Taking back his ace.)* Better not... *(After scratching his head a moment, he picks up the opponent's hand again and removes a card, replacing it with one of his own.)* There! Now I've got the ten of diamonds!... *(Playing his ace.)* Building ten... *(Playing a card from the opponent's hand.)* Very good... *(Taking the trick, triumphantly.)* My trick! Four points, monsieur!

(MADAME DE CHAMPRINET enters from LEONIE's room.)

MADAME DE CHAMPRINET: Ah, Gustave... *(Looking around.)* You're all alone?

DE CHAMPRINET *(laying down the cards):* Yes... Your Monsieur Ennepèque is off changing his pants.

MADAME DE CHAMPRINET: Is that all he can think of at a time like this? When his wife is in labor!... Why? What was wrong with the ones he was wearing?

DE CHAMPRINET: He wet them.

MADAME DE CHAMPRINET: He didn't!

DE CHAMPRINET: That is, the midwife wet them.

MADAME DE CHAMPRINET: She what?... Frau Grossfinger... Was she sitting on his lap?

DE CHAMPRINET *(guffawing):* Good God, no!... With a basin of water!

MADAME DE CHAMPRINET: Oh...

(She sits down across from him.)

DE CHAMPRINET *(still chuckling):* So... How is she?

MADAME DE CHAMPRINET: Frau Grossfinger?... Carrying on...

DE CHAMPRINET: No, no! Léonie!... Frau Grossfinger be damned!

MADAME DE CHAMPRINET: Well... *(Sighing.)* She's coming along...

(They pause for a long moment, looking at one another, MADAME DE CHAMPRINET *nodding ponderously,* DE CHAMPRINET *shaking his head.)*

DE CHAMPRINET *(breaking the silence):* We needed this, didn't we! Married eight months... Lovely!

(He gets up.)

MADAME DE CHAMPRINET: I know... I know...

DE CHAMPRINET: Tsk tsk tsk! *(Crossing left, pacing.)* You can thank your monsieur Hector Ennepèque!

MADAME DE CHAMPRINET: My Monsieur—

DE CHAMPRINET: It's a scandal!

MADAME DE CHAMPRINET: My... Why my—

DE CHAMPRINET: Why? Who pushed her into the arms of that twit? Not me!

MADAME DE CHAMPRINET: "Pushed"? Hardly!

DE CHAMPRINET: Well then, "nudged"!... I loathed him from the beginning!

MADAME DE CHAMPRINET: Yes! Just like all the others! If you'd had your way, Gustave, she'd never have married anyone! Ennepèque was no bargain, but she wasn't getting any younger!

DE CHAMPRINET *(crossing back right, standing behind the bridge table):* I'm sorry, I can't help it! It's just that... *(Waxing sentimental.)* You have one daughter, the apple of your eye... A perfect little angel... And there's nothing too good for her, nothing you wouldn't do to make her a fine young lady... Always setting the best example, never raising your voice... Never acting middle-class...

MADAME DE CHAMPRINET *(nodding):* I know...

DE CHAMPRINET: Then one fine day... *(Snapping his fingers.)* A man comes along... *(Gradually raising his voice.)* A total stranger! Someone you don't even know! *(At the table.)* And that's that! One two three! She's gone!... Next thing you know... *(Pounding the table with his fist, almost shouting.)* He's sleeping with her, for heaven's sake! And there's nothing you can do about it! Nothing! Just accept it! *(Standing over the table, across from her.)* Can you sit there and tell me that that's not revolting?

MADAME DE CHAMPRINET: But Gustave... That's marriage...

DE CHAMPRINET *(pacing left):* Bah! You wouldn't understand!... You've never been a father!

MADAME DE CHAMPRINET *(continuing her thought):* Besides... I hate to admit it, but he does have a good point or two...

DE CHAMPRINET *(stopping and glaring at her):* You're not serious!

MADAME DE CHAMPRINET: I'd never tell him so to his face, but—

DE CHAMPRINET *(returning to the bridge table):* For example?

MADAME DE CHAMPRINET: Well, he does give in to her least little whim...

DE CHAMPRINET: I should hope so! She's a De Champrinet! What the devil is he?

MADAME DE CHAMPRINET *(continuing):* Even when... Sometimes, you know, a pregnant woman can be difficult...

DE CHAMPRINET: Not my Léonie!

MADAME DE CHAMPRINET: Oh... A little... Why, just now, before you got here... *(Smiling.)* It was priceless! You should have seen...

DE CHAMPRINET: What?

MADAME DE CHAMPRINET *(with a gesture toward where the action took place):* Well, there she was, insisting that... You'll never believe it!... that she wanted him to wear that chamber pot!

(She points to the pot, on the floor by the console table.)

DE CHAMPRINET: Wear it? Where!

MADAME DE CHAMPRINET: On his head!

DE CHAMPRINET: And he did?

(He sits down across from her.)

MADAME DE CHAMPRINET: Yes! It was absolutely priceless!

DE CHAMPRINET: I told you that son-in-law of yours was a twit!

MADAME DE CHAMPRINET: I know... But he did it to make her happy. Some husbands wouldn't care...

DE CHAMPRINET: I wish I could have seen it! It would have made my day!... *(As an afterthought.)* Was it empty?

MADAME DE CHAMPRINET: Of course! It's Jean-Jacques's little potty...

DE CHAMPRINET: Whose?

MADAME DE CHAMPRINET: Jean-Jacques.

DE CHAMPRINET: Rousseau?

MADAME DE CHAMPRINET: No, no!... The baby!

DE CHAMPRINET *(nodding):* Oh... Yes, the baby... *(Returning to his* idée fixe, *picking up his hand of cards.)* Eight months... Eight months... *(Absentmindedly.)* Go ahead... Your play...

MADAME DE CHAMPRINET: My what?

DE CHAMPRINET: I just took a trick with your ten of diamonds... *(Correcting.)* My ten...

MADAME DE CHAMPRINET: What "ten..."? I'm not playing cards!

DE CHAMPRINET *(realizing his lapse):* Cards?... No, no... I mean... *(Shaking his head, sighing.)* Tsk tsk tsk!... Eight months...

MADAME DE CHAMPRINET: I know...

(ENNEPEQUE enters from the hall with a complete change of clothes.)

DE CHAMPRINET: Speak of the devil...

(As ENNEPEQUE putters about nervously at the chest of drawers, up left, LEONIE's door opens and MADAME GROSSFINGER steps out.)

MADAME GROSSFINGER *(at the door, to DE CHAMPRINET):* You go in now, ja!... Madame wants to see her papa... *(To MADAME DE CHAMPRINET.)* Und her mamma...

DE CHAMPRINET: Ah!

MADAME DE CHAMPRINET *(simultaneously):* Poor lamb!

(The both get up. DE CHAMPRINET rushes to the door, with MADAME DE CHAMPRINET close behind.)

MADAME GROSSFINGER *(barring the entrance, to DE CHAMPRINET):* But just for a minute, you hear? In und out!

DE CHAMPRINET *(pushing her aside, impatiently):* Yes, yes! *(Under his breath.)* Old battle-axe!

MADAME GROSSFINGER *(to DE CHAMPRINET, as he and MADAME DE CHAMPRINET reach the open door, clutching her bosom):* Monsieur!

DE CHAMPRINET *(exiting into the wings):* Well now, pigeon...

MADAME DE CHAMPRINET *(following him out, simultaneously):* Feeling better, treasure?

(The door closes.)

MADAME GROSSFINGER *(sitting down to the left of the bridge table):* Some men! They couldn't keep their hands off a woman!

(She begins absentmindedly playing with the cards.)

ENNEPEQUE *(approaching her, a little timidly):* Madame... Is she coming along?

MADAME GROSSFINGER *(without turning to look at him, with a non-committal sigh):* Huhuhu...

ENNEPEQUE: My wife...

MADAME GROSSFINGER: Pfff...

ENNEPEQUE: Is that yes or no?

MADAME GROSSFINGER: Hmmm...

ENNEPEQUE *(nodding, still in the dark):* Aha...

MADAME GROSSFINGER *(facing him, categorically):* You ask, so I tell you! I would expect, by now, more dilation...

ENNEPEQUE *(trying to appear knowledgeable):* More... Yes, so would I...

MADAME GROSSFINGER: You? What do you know?

ENNEPEQUE: I mean... I suppose—

MADAME GROSSFINGER: Ja... More I would expect... But... *(She makes a small circle with her thumb and forefinger and, squinting, holds it up to her eye, gesturing with it twice.)*

ENNEPEQUE: Oh, well. More would have been nice, but... As long as everything is... *(He duplicates her gesture—thumb and forefinger touching, other fingers extended—mistaking it for the common sign for "Perfect!")* Then there's nothing to worry about?

MADAME GROSSFINGER: Worry? No... It just takes a little longer... *(Getting up.)* Und especially mit a few things I couldn't quite explain...

ENNEPEQUE: Oh?

MADAME GROSSFINGER *(in her professional tone):* Ja... When I palpate... *(Feeling an imaginary belly.)* So... It's hard to tell exactly what position... *(*ENNEPEQUE *nods.)* Of course, that would be only maybe a little hydroamniosis...

ENNEPEQUE: I wouldn't be surprised...

MADAME GROSSFINGER: Mit a touch of edema... But two points I find, plain as day... *(Poking him in the ribs.)* Here... Und here!

ENNEPEQUE *(waiting for her conclusion):* And?

MADAME GROSSFINGER: Und it could be a geminate gestation, I suppose.

(She sits down again to the left of the bridge table.)

ENNEPEQUE *(leaning over her):* Beg pardon?

MADAME GROSSFINGER: A geminate gestation... *(Enunciating.)* Geminate... She has some in her family? Or in yours, maybe?

ENNEPEQUE: Well... Not that I know of... My father is a Scorpio and my mother is a Leo. I'm not sure about hers...

MADAME GROSSFINGER: Your what? What are you talking... *(Standing up.)* Geminate... That means twins!

ENNEPEQUE *(with a start):* Twins?... *(Moving center.)* She can't... Two cribs! Two... Two everything!

MADAME GROSSFINGER *(moving right):* Ja! It's possible...

ENNEPEQUE: Six dozen diapers!

MADAME GROSSFINGER: But I couldn't be sure... *(Sitting to the right of the bridge table.)* Did she have a shtethoscopy?

ENNEPEQUE *(returning right):* Did she... *(Hesitating.)* No... Not that I... *(Sitting down across from her.)* But she did have a sitz bath this morning...

MADAME GROSSFINGER: She what?... What connection...? It's like, if I ask you "Do you get a lot of colds?", und you tell me: "No, but I like to wear lederhosen..."

ENNEPEQUE: Sorry...

MADAME GROSSFINGER *(getting up, under her breath):* Shtupid!

ENNEPEQUE: I thought it was important...

MADAME GROSSFINGER: Because, if she did... Well, mit the shtethoscope I could tell from the heartbeats.

ENNEPEQUE: Oh...

MADAME GROSSFINGER *(very matter-of-fact):* Now, of course, it could be a left posterior sacro-lumbar... Mit foetal inversion... In other words, a breech...

ENNEPEQUE: A breech?

MADAME GROSSFINGER: Ja! *(Moving up to the dining table.)* Obviously!

(She snatches a crust of bread.)

ENNEPEQUE *(reaching out, grabbing the back of her coat, pulling her back):* Just a minute!

MADAME GROSSFINGER: Please?

ENNEPEQUE: This... This "breech"... Is that good?

MADAME GROSSFINGER *(nibbling the bread):* Good? *(Laughing at his obvious stupidity.)* Ha ha ha!... Better I'd have a cranial parturition any day! Wouldn't you?

ENNEPEQUE: Oh... Any day... Any day...

MADAME GROSSFINGER: Of course, a right or left occipito-lumbar... Anterior or posterior...

ENNEPEQUE: Yes, yes... Never mind!

MADAME GROSSFINGER *(moving left to the easy chair as she speaks):* Such shtrange cases we see nowadays in our profession!

ENNEPEQUE: Yes, I'm sure...

MADAME GROSSFINGER *(sitting down):* Ja!... Why, just the other day, one of my patients... In her eighth month, also... She had a mole...

ENNEPEQUE *(with a start):* My God! Can that happen?... *(Aside.)* A mole?

MADAME GROSSFINGER: Ja! *(Pointing to her thighs.)* Here!... A big one...

ENNEPEQUE *(relieved):* Oh... A mole...

MADAME GROSSFINGER *(sitting back, with an air of professional satisfaction):* A condyloma...

ENNEPEQUE *(repeating, mechanically):* Condyloma...

MADAME GROSSFINGER: A nevus, monsieur!... A hydatiform nevus... Like a big bunch of blueberries...

(She continues nibbling.)

ENNEPEQUE *(aside):* That I understand!

MADAME GROSSFINGER: Such shtrange cases nowadays...

ENNEPEQUE *(aside):* Old windbag!

MADAME GROSSFINGER: So shtrange...

ENNEPEQUE *(getting up, going over to her, rebelling against her show of erudition, aloud):* Yes, well... Believe me, I've seen stranger!

MADAME GROSSFINGER: You? Shtranger than a hydatiform nevus, monsieur?

ENNEPEQUE: Yes! But you probably wouldn't know...

MADAME GROSSFINGER *(sitting up straight, categorically):* Of course I would! What is it?

ENNEPEQUE: A...*(Deliberately.)* A nephro-mixo-ilio-sacroloma.

MADAME GROSSFINGER: A what?

ENNEPEQUE *(trying to repeat):* A nephro-ilio-sacro-mixoloma... And in the seventh month!

MADAME GROSSFINGER *(reflecting for a moment):* Ja, ja! That could happen!

ENNEPEQUE: Oh? You've seen cases?

MADAME GROSSFINGER: Not many... But... Ja, a few...

ENNEPEQUE *(with a nod):* Aha...

MADAME GROSSFINGER *(getting up):* A few...

ENNEPEQUE: I'm sure...

MADAME GROSSFINGER *(happy to change the subject):* So! When do I eat? What happened to my dinner?

(She moves toward the dining table.)

ENNEPEQUE: Just a minute, I'll find out... *(Crossing up to the kitchen door, aside.)* "A few" my foot!

MADAME GROSSFINGER: A horse I could eat!

ENNEPEQUE *(under his breath):* That doesn't surprise me! *(Opening the door, calling.)* Antoinette! You can serve now!...

(DE CHAMPRINET enters from LEONIE's room.)

MADAME GROSSFINGER *(noticing him):* You!... What took so long? I said: "In und out!"... Naughty, naughty!

DE CHAMPRINET: I know... But when I saw her, poor child... How much longer...?

MADAME GROSSFINGER *(with a shrug):* Who knows?

DE CHAMPRINET: Well, if *you* don't...

ENNEPEQUE *(to DE CHAMPRINET, authoritatively, coming center):* We would have expected more elation by now...

DE CHAMPRINET: What?

ENNEPEQUE: But it could just be a foetal diversion...

DE CHAMPRINET *(glaring at him):* What are you talking about?

ENNEPEQUE: Of course, a cranial partition would be better! *(To MADAME GROSSFINGER.)* Right?

DE CHAMPRINET *(to MADAME GROSSFINGER):* What is he—

ENNEPEQUE *(triumphantly):* And it may even be a germanic gestation! *(Aside.)* So there!

MADAME GROSSFINGER *(to ENNEPEQUE, correcting):* Geminate!... Geminate!...

DE CHAMPRINET *(to ENNEPEQUE, suddenly understanding, shocked):* Twins?

ENNEPEQUE *(to DE CHAMPRINET, deflated):* You know?

DE CHAMPRINET *(to MADAME GROSSFINGER):* Twins, madame?

MADAME GROSSFINGER *(with a vague wave of the hand):* Possible... It could be...

(ANTOINETTE appears at the kitchen door carrying a tray with the rest of the macaroni and the salad, as well as a bottle of champagne.)

ANTOINETTE *(putting the things on the sideboard, to MADAME GROSSFINGER):* Madame's dinner is ready.

MADAME GROSSFINGER: Ah!

ANTOINETTE *(to DE CHAMPRINET):* And monsieur's too...

(During the ensuing dialogue, she takes the new settings from the sideboard and sets the table.)

MADAME GROSSFINGER *(to* DE CHAMPRINET*)*: You're joining me? How nice!... *(Taking him under her arm.)* Come, Monsieur Champrinet...

DE CHAMPRINET *(correcting)*: De... De...

MADAME GROSSFINGER: Please?

DE CHAMPRINET *(emphasizing)*: *De* Champrinet, madame!

MADAME GROSSFINGER: So... Come...

DE CHAMPRINET *(with exaggerated deference)*: Your word is my command!

(They move to the dining table as ENNEPEQUE *settles into the easy chair.)*

MADAME GROSSFINGER *(sitting to the right)*: I sit here. You take the side mit the draft...

DE CHAMPRINET *(with a little bow)*: Too kind!

(They sit down across from each other as ANTOINETTE *finishes setting the table.)*

MADAME GROSSFINGER *(to* ANTOINETTE*:)* Mademoiselle... You shtay mit madame while I eat, ja? Und you call if she needs me.

ANTOINETTE *(right)*: But madame's dinner...

MADAME GROSSFINGER: No, no... Just put it down und run along!

ANTOINETTE *(getting the food from the sideboard and putting it on the dining table)*: Well, if madame is sure...

MADAME GROSSFINGER: If we need something... *(Pointing to* ENNEPEQUE, *in the easy chair.)* He can do!

(ANTOINETTE comes down right and knocks on the door.)

MADAME DE CHAMPRINET's VOICE: Come in!

(ANTOINETTE exits.)

MADAME GROSSFINGER *(making herself comfortable)*: There! *(To* DE CHAMPRINET.*)* Cozy, ja?

DE CHAMPRINET *(serving himself some salad)*: Yes... Isn't it...

MADAME GROSSFINGER: It reminds me of London... *(Serving herself some macaroni.)* When I dined mit Lord Athol. *(She pronounces the name with a long "o".)*

(She passes him the platter.)

DE CHAMPRINET *(pronouncing the name correctly, with a short "o")*: You and Lord Athol?... *(Taking the macaroni.)* Thank you... *(He serves himself.)*

MADAME GROSSFINGER: Ja, while his wife was in labor... *(Mispronouncing.)* Lady Athol...

DE CHAMPRINET: Aha... *(Offering her the salad.)* Salad?

MADAME GROSSFINGER: No, thank you.
(She attacks the macaroni, taking a heaping forkful.)

DE CHAMPRINET: You took care of the delivery?
(He begins eating it too.)

MADAME GROSSFINGER: Oh... I had a hand in it, ja...

DE CHAMPRINET *(eating):* I see... I see...

MADAME GROSSFINGER *(grimacing at the taste):* That was nice und cozy too...

DE CHAMPRINET *(grimacing likewise):* The delivery?

MADAME GROSSFINGER: No, monsieur... The dinner! Very cozy... *(With a pointed look in* ENNEPEQUE'S *direction.)* Und plenty servants he had! Not like here!

ENNEPEQUE *(from the easy chair, to* MADAME GROSSFINGER, *sarcastically):* I'm sorry! If I'd known you were coming for dinner...

MADAME GROSSFINGER: Pfff! *(Holding out the champagne bottle to him.)* Here! Do something!

ENNEPEQUE: Me?

MADAME GROSSFINGER: Who else? Monsieur und I are dining!

ENNEPEQUE *(getting up, resigned):* Of course! I should have guessed...
(He takes the bottle and crosses right to the chair against the wall, outside of LEONIE'S *room, grumbling as he sits down. During the following exchange, he tries unsuccessfully to uncork the bottle.)*

MADAME GROSSFINGER *(reminiscing, still grimacing at the macaroni):* Ja... *(Mispronouncing.)* Lord Athol...

DE CHAMPRINET: Pleasant chap... For an Englishman...
(He risks another forkful.)

MADAME GROSSFINGER: You know him?

DE CHAMPRINET *(grimacing):* We've met... When you travel in the right circles...

MADAME GROSSFINGER: Ja, ja!... You must all know each other, I suppose. All you De Champrinets... All you Athols... *(She continues to mispronounce.)* Und what are you, monsieur? A count?

DE CHAMPRINET *(modestly):* Well... As a matter of fact...

(He puts down his fork and pushes away his plate.)

MADAME GROSSFINGER *(impressed)*: Oh! A count!... A real one! *(Musing as she eats.)* But... Then... How come madame... Your daughter... *(Glancing up at* ENNEPEQUE.*)* How come she married someone who's... *(Hiccuping.)* Hoop!... nothing?

ENNEPEQUE *(still struggling with the bottle)*: I heard that!

MADAME GROSSFINGER *(clapping her hand to her mouth)*: I beg your pardon!

DE CHAMPRINET *(ignoring* ENNEPEQUE *completely, to* MADAME GROSSFINGER, *sighing)*: Hindsight is better than foresight, madame!

MADAME GROSSFINGER *(still reluctantly eating)*: Ja, that's true!... Hoop! *(Embarrassed, pointing to the macaroni.)* Shtrong, ja?

DE CHAMPRINET: Very!

MADAME GROSSFINGER: Hoop!... It gives hiccups!

DE CHAMPRINET: So I see!

MADAME GROSSFINGER: Ja!... Hoop!... Not you?

DE CHAMPRINET: Me? No... Never...

MADAME GROSSFINGER: You're lucky!... Hoop! *(To* ENNE-PEQUE.*)* So? How long are you... Hoop!... taking?

ENNEPEQUE: It's the damned cork! It's stuck!... If you think it's so damned easy...

(MADAME GROSSFINGER picks up the water pitcher but finds it empty. She continues hiccuping.)

DE CHAMPRINET *(to* ENNEPEQUE*)*: Monsieur! I'll thank you to keep a civil tongue in your... Hoop!... Damn! *(He covers his mouth.)* Now I've got them!... Hoop!... *(Getting up, to* ENNE-PEQUE.*)* Give me that! You... You... Hoop!

MADAME GROSSFINGER *(to* DE CHAMPRINET*)*: Never, monsieur?

ENNEPEQUE *(getting up and bringing the bottle to* DE CHAM-PRINET*)*: With pleasure! It's all yours!

MADAME GROSSFINGER *(getting up and moving down right, to* DE CHAMPRINET*)*: Please! Hoop!... Please! Hurry!...

(For several moments, DE CHAMPRINET, *sitting at the dining table, struggles unsuccessfully with the cork, as* MADAME GROSSFINGER, *down right, and* ENNEPEQUE, *standing between them, look on in silence broken only by a counterpoint of hiccups.)*

DE CHAMPRINET: Hoop!

MADAME GROSSFINGER: Hoop! Hoop!

DE CHAMPRINET: Hoop!

(A pause.)

MADAME GROSSFINGER: Hoop!

DE CHAMPRINET: Hoop! Hoop!

MADAME GROSSFINGER: Hoop! *(To* DE CHAMPRINET, *losing patience.)* So?

DE CHAMPRINET: It's the cork... It's... It's...

ENNEPEQUE *(down right, to* MADAME GROSSFINGER*):* "Shtuck!" *(To* DE CHAMPRINET.*)* Yes, Count!... Isn't it!

*(*DE CHAMPRINET *and* MADAME GROSSFINGER *continue the following together, duplicating the rhythm of a moment before.)*

DE CHAMPRINET: Hoop!... Hoop! Hoop!... Hoop!

MADAME GROSSFINGER: Hoop!... Hoop! Hoop!... Hoop!

(A pause.)

DE CHAMPRINET: Hoop!... Hoop! Hoop!... Hoop!

MADAME GROSSFINGER: Hoop!... Hoop! Hoop!... Hoop!

DE CHAMPRINET *(slamming the bottle down on the table):* Damn!

ENNEPEQUE: Tsk tsk tsk!

MADAME GROSSFINGER *(to* DE CHAMPRINET*):* Water!... Hoop!... Anything! *(Pointing to the console table.)* There!... The bottle of... Hoop! dishtilled water!

DE CHAMPRINET: Ah!... Good!... Hoop!

(He gets up and crosses quickly left, and picks up one of the bottles.)

MADAME GROSSFINGER *(moving to the dining table, watching):* Nein!... No, no!... Hoop!... Not the mercury chloride! *(Pointing.)* That one!... Hoop!... That one! *(As* DE CHAMPRINET *picks up the right bottle.)* Ja!

DE CHAMPRINET *(coming to the dining table with the bottle):* Hoop!... Hoop!

(He fills her glass.)

MADAME GROSSFINGER: Ja!... So!... Hoop!

(She drinks, as he fills his own glass and drinks.)

DE CHAMPRINET: Ah!... Hoop!

(They take several more drinks, as the hiccups gradually subside.)

MADAME GROSSFINGER *(sighing):* Ah!... That's better!

(She sits down to the right of the dining table.)

DE CHAMPRINET *(with a deep breath):* Much!

(Just as MADAME GROSSFINGER *sits down,* LEONIE's *door opens and* MADAME DE CHAMPRINET *rushes out.)*

MADAME DE CHAMPRINET: Madame... Frau... Madame Grossfinger...

MADAME DE CHAMPRINET *(casually correcting): De* Grossfinger...

MADAME DE CHAMPRINET: Yes, yes... Please! I think you should come...

MADAME GROSSFINGER *(getting up):* Ah?

DE CHAMPRINET *(approaching, to* MADAME DE CHAMPRINET*):* Is something wrong?

ENNEPEQUE *(behind the bridge table, to* MADAME DE CHAMPRINET*):* What's the matter?

MADAME DE CHAMPRINET *(ignoring* ENNEPEQUE, *to* DE CHAMPRINET*):* No, no... But I think she should come have a look.

MADAME GROSSFINGER: Ja, ja! Right away! *(Moving toward* LEONIE's *room, with* MADAME DE CHAMPRINET *at her heels, to* ENNEPEQUE.) Und you... Make me some coffee!

ENNEPEQUE: What?

MADAME GROSSFINGER *(at the threshold):* Coffee! *(Turning to exit.)* Hoop! *(Under her breath.)* Gott in Himmel! Noch einmal?

(She exits, followed by MADAME DE CHAMPRINET.)

ENNEPEQUE *(pacing up left, imitating):* "Make me some coffee! Make me..." *(To* DE CHAMPRINET.) What does she think I am, her maid?

DE CHAMPRINET: Good idea... I'll have some too. No sugar... *(He sits down in the easy chair.)*

ENNEPEQUE *(speechless):* You... Oh!... *(Beginning to lose patience.)* And will there be anything else for monsieur?

DE CHAMPRINET: No, no... Just the coffee...

*(*ANTOINETTE *enters quickly from* LEONIE's *room.)*

ENNEPEQUE *(calling to her):* Antoinette!

ANTOINETTE *(without stopping):* Monsieur?

ENNEPEQUE *(snapping his fingers):* Coffee! And make it quick!

ANTOINETTE *(pushing him out of the way):* No time, monsieur! *(She exits to the kitchen.)*

ENNEPEQUE *(watching her go):* Of course! How silly of me! *(To* DE CHAMPRINET.) Sorry! She has no time, monsieur!... Later! You'll have to wait...

(He moves to the dining table, leaning against it, almost sitting, arms folded.)

DE CHAMPRINET *(taking a cigarette from his cigarette case, annoyed):* Lovely!... What a day!... *(Looking toward* LEONIE'*s room.)* My daughter... That supper... The hiccups... And now no coffee!... Lovely!

(He lights the cigarette.)

ENNEPEQUE: My sympathies!

DE CHAMPRINET *(getting up, pacing nervously):* Your sympathies!... Don't bother! *(Under his breath.)* I should have had my head examined! A De Champrinet and that!... *(He continues pacing and grumbling for a moment; then, standing in front of* ENNE-PEQUE, *back to the audience.)* And how are you going to feed him? Have you thought of that, monsieur?

ENNEPEQUE: Feed him?

DE CHAMPRINET *(impatiently):* Yes! *(Putting his hands to his chest and lifting a pair of imaginary breasts.)* Feed him!... Who's going to?

ENNEPEQUE: His mother, monsieur! *(Sarcastically.)* I would if I could...

DE CHAMPRINET *(with a start):* His mother? My... You don't expect her to...

(He repeats the gesture.)

ENNEPEQUE: Why not? A lot of women nurse their own babies.

DE CHAMPRINET: A lot of peasants, you mean! Not our kind, monsieur!

ENNEPEQUE *(with a wave of the hand):* Pfff!

DE CHAMPRINET *(moving right):* I didn't give you my daughter's hand so that you could turn her into a... a pump! Not a De Champrinet, monsieur!

ENNEPEQUE: Excuse me... An Ennepèque!

DE CHAMPRINET *(glancing over his shoulder):* Oh là là!... "An Ennepèque" indeed! *(Sitting to the right of the bridge table.)* How chic!

ENNEPEQUE *(turning aside, disgustedly):* Bah!

DE CHAMPRINET: And just because he's too cheap to hire a wetnurse! *(Turning toward* ENNEPEQUE.*)* Or to buy a baby bottle!

ENNEPEQUE: A bottle? No thank you! Too many bottle babies turn out to be runts!

DE CHAMPRINET *(half-standing, with a little bow):* I was a bottle baby, monsieur!

(He sits back down.)

ENNEPEQUE *(giving him tit for tat):* Then you know what I mean!

DE CHAMPRINET *(ignoring the remark):* The idea! To expect my daughter to nurse!

ENNEPEQUE *(more and more on edge):* For goodness' sake! The baby isn't born yet! First things first!

DE CHAMPRINET *(sarcastically):* Ask her for the milk in your coffee, why don't you?

ENNEPEQUE: Monsieur! That's disgusting!

(LEONIE's door opens and MADAME GROSSFINGER comes storming out.)

MADAME GROSSFINGER: The maid!... Where is she?

DE CHAMPRINET: What's the matter?

ENNEPEQUE *(simultaneously):* What's wrong? What is it?

MADAME GROSSFINGER *(making a beeline for the kitchen door, half-opening it, calling):* Adèlè!... Adèlè!...

ENNEPEQUE *(to MADAME GROSSFINGER):* You're wasting your breath! Her name is Antoinette!

DE CHAMPRINET *(to MADAME GROSSFINGER, repeating):* What's the matter?

MADAME GROSSFINGER *(to ENNEPEQUE):* Ah... So... I'm confusing mit the Athols. *(She continues to mispronounce.)*

ENNEPEQUE *(appalled):* With what?

MADAME GROSSFINGER *(calling):* Antoinette!

DE CHAMPRINET *(to MADAME GROSSFINGER, insisting):* What's wrong?

(ANTOINETTE appears at the kitchen door.)

DE CHAMPRINET *(to MADAME GROSSFINGER):* Madame...

ANTOINETTE *(to MADAME GROSSFINGER):* Madame called?

MADAME GROSSFINGER: Ja! Please... A hot water bottle!... Und hurry!

ANTOINETTE: Yes, madame.

(ANTOINETTE exits to the kitchen.)

ENNEPEQUE *(grabbing MADAME GROSSFINGER by the arm):* Madame...

DE CHAMPRINET: Madame...

ENNEPEQUE *(pulling her down center):* What is it? Is something happening?

MADAME GROSSFINGER: Happening? Oh, ja! Something's happening! You could say!

DE CHAMPRINET *(getting up, joining them):* Well? What is it?

ENNEPEQUE *(simultaneously, insistent)*: Tell me! Tell me!

MADAME GROSSFINGER *(between the two men):* It's all over, that's what!

ENNEPEQUE *(breaking out in a smile, with a sigh of relief):* It is?

MADAME GROSSFINGER *(turning to* ENNEPEQUE*):* Oh, ja!

DE CHAMPRINET: Already?

MADAME GROSSFINGER *(turning to* DE CHAMPRINET*):* Ja, ja!

ENNEPEQUE *(expectantly):* And it's a boy!

MADAME GROSSFINGER *(turning):* No!

DE CHAMPRINET: A girl!

MADAME GROSSFINGER *(turning):* No!

ENNEPEQUE *(slapping his forehead with the heel of his hand):* Don't tell me!... It's twins!

MADAME GROSSFINGER *(turning):* No... It isn't!

DE CHAMPRINET: It isn't?

ENNEPEQUE *(to* MADAME GROSSFINGER*):* Then...

MADAME GROSSFINGER *(emphasizing):* It isn't!

ENNEPEQUE: Isn't what?

MADAME GROSSFINGER: Isn't... Period!... *(Very professional.)* It's a pseudocyesis!

ENNEPEQUE: A what?

DE CHAMPRINET *(simultaneously):* A what?

MADAME GROSSFINGER *(to* ENNEPEQUE*):* False pregnancy... *(To* DE CHAMPRINET.*)* Hysterical...

ENNEPEQUE: But...

MADAME GROSSFINGER: Nerves... *(Gesturing.)* Poof!... Nothing!

ENNEPEQUE: But... But... But...

DE CHAMPRINET *(simultaneously):* Nerves?... Just nerves?

ENNEPEQUE: All those labor pains...

MADAME GROSSFINGER: Gas!

ENNEPEQUE: But—

DE CHAMPRINET: Nerves?

MADAME GROSSFINGER *(disengaging herself, moving toward the bridge table):* Ja! It happens... We all make mistakes. No one's perfect...

ENNEPEQUE *(with a deflating gasp):* Oh!

DE CHAMPRINET *(simultaneously):* Oh!

MADAME GROSSFINGER: I saw once a woman carry for twenty-five months. People began to wonder... "It can't be an elephant," they said. Und one fine day, poof!... Just like in the fable...

ENNEPEQUE *(dejectedly):* Fable?

DE CHAMPRINET: What fable?

MADAME GROSSFINGER *(to* DE CHAMPRINET*):* The one all us midwives know by heart, monsieur. "The Mountain That Gave Birth to a Mouse."

ENNEPEQUE *(still not quite comprehending):* "The mountain..."

MADAME GROSSFINGER *(to* ENNEPEQUE*):* Madame Ennepèque is just making like the mountain...

ENNEPEQUE *(timidly):* She... She's having a mouse?

DE CHAMPRINET: What?

MADAME GROSSFINGER *(laughing, to* ENNEPEQUE*):* No, monsieur! *(Picking up the cards from the bridge table, holding them out to him.)* Misdeal!... Sorry! You try again, ja?

ENNEPEQUE *(falling into the easy chair, disconsolately):* Misdeal!... Mis—

DE CHAMPRINET *(to* ENNEPEQUE, *furious):* Congratulations! You... Can't you do anything right? You...

ENNEPEQUE: What?

DE CHAMPRINET: You... Not even a simple thing like a baby! Good God? I should have known!

ENNEPEQUE: But whose fault, for goodness' sake...

DE CHAMPRINET *(ranting):* "Whose fault" indeed! Of course! Tell me it's not yours! You had nothing to do with it! Nothing! Nothing!

ENNEPEQUE: I didn't say that, but—

MADAME GROSSFINGER *(trying to come between them, to* ENNEPEQUE*):* Monsieur!... *(To* DE CHAMPRINET.*)* Monsieur!...

DE CHAMPRINET *(to* MADAME GROSSFINGER, *turning her around sharply and pushing her right):* Oh dry up! You...

MADAME GROSSFINGER *(shocked):* Monsieur!

*(*LEONIE*'s door opens and* MADAME DE CHAMPRINET *makes a beeline for* DE CHAMPRINET, *obviously distraught.)*

MADAME DE CHAMPRINET *(to* DE CHAMPRINET*):* Hysterical pregnancy!... Nerves!... Did you ever see...?

DE CHAMPRINET: That's your son-in-law for you!

ENNEPEQUE: But—

MADAME DE CHAMPRINET *(continuing her lament):* Nerves... And gas!

DE CHAMPRINET *(to* MADAME DE CHAMPRINET*):* Your Monsieur Ennepèque!

ENNEPEQUE: Now just one minute—

MADAME DE CHAMPRINET *(to* DE CHAMPRINET*):* If we only knew before...

DE CHAMPRINET: But I told you! I told you a hundred times: "He's not one of us! He's just not our kind..."

ENNEPEQUE *(to* DE CHAMPRINET, *finally exploding):* Your kind! Your kind!... *(Slapping under his chin with the back of his hand.)* I've had it up to here with your kind, goddammit!

MADAME DE CHAMPRINET: Monsieur!

ENNEPEQUE *(to* MADAME DE CHAMPRINET, *pointing to* LEONIE*'s room, shouting):* It's her nerves! And her gas!... And her hysterics!... So blame her, why don't you!... Oh no! She's "your kind!"

MADAME GROSSFINGER *(to* ENNEPEQUE*):* Please, monsieur! Shhh! *(Pointing to* LEONIE*'s room.)* Madame—

ENNEPEQUE: Oh, shut up!

MADAME GROSSFINGER: Oh!

(She withdraws discreetly down right, out of the line of fire.)

ENNEPEQUE *(pacing):* My fault! All mine!... First you blame me because she's having a baby! Now you blame me because she isn't! Damn it, make up your mind!

(He arrives by the console table.)

MADAME DE CHAMPRINET *(to* ENNEPEQUE, *moving toward him):* Monsieur!... If you could see how ridiculous you're acting...

DE CHAMPRINET *(to* MADAME DE CHAMPRINET*):* He can't help it! He is!

(He sits down to the left of the bridge table.)

ENNEPEQUE *(to* MADAME DE CHAMPRINET*):* Yes! Like all of *(Emphasizing.)* my kind!

DE CHAMPRINET *(snidely):* Quite!

ENNEPEQUE: Well, that's just fine with me!

MADAME DE CHAMPRINET: Of course! I'm not surprised! A man who parades around with a baby's potty on his head—

ENNEPEQUE *(seething):* What?

MADAME DE CHAMPRINET *(sneering):* You heard me!

ENNEPEQUE *(trying desperately to control himself):* Oh!... That's enough! *(Striding up toward the hall door.)* Before I do something I'll be sorry for...

MADAME DE CHAMPRINET *(running to pick up the chamber pot by the console table):* Wait, monsieur! *(Holding it out to him behind his back.)* Your hat!

ENNEPEQUE *(at the door, turning and snatching it out of her hand):* Yes! Thank you! My hat!

(He comes down toward the dining table and holds it above his head with both hands as if about to smash it to bits on the floor.)

DE CHAMPRINET *(still sitting, to* ENNEPEQUE, *quickly):* No, no! Please!... Please! Don't!... *(*ENNEPEQUE *takes a deep breath as if to control himself, and is about to lay the pot down on the dining table.)* Put it on!

ENNEPEQUE: What?

DE CHAMPRINET: Put it on! Just so I can say I've seen it...

MADAME GROSSFINGER *(still down right, clapping her hands):* Oh ja! Ja, ja!

DE CHAMPRINET *(to* ENNEPEQUE*):* Because you must be the first man ever to wear a chamber pot!

ENNEPEQUE: Oh, really?

DE CHAMPRINET *(with a nasty chuckle):* I imagine...

ENNEPEQUE: Well, I may be the first, but... *(Picking up the pot and approaching* DE CHAMPRINET *at the bridge table.)* Your Highness is the second!

(He plants it tightly on DE CHAMPRINET's *head.)*
(The following three exclamations are simultaneous.)

DE CHAMPRINET: Oh!

MADAME DE CHAMPRINET: Oh!

MADAME GROSSFINGER: Oh!

(There is a general uproar, with appropriate exclamations, as ENNEPEQUE *stands, hands on hips, watching the others try unsuccessfully to remove the pot from* DE CHAMPRINET's *head. After a few moments,* ANTOINETTE *enters from the kitchen with a hot water bottle.)*

ANTOINETTE: Here's the hot water—

(At the sight before her, she drops the bottle with a little scream.)

ENNEPEQUE: Maybe now I'll get some respect in this house!

(He turns on his heel, crosses up left, and storms out the hall door, as the bedlam continues, and the curtain falls.)

CURTAIN

"FIVE SPLENDID PLAYS... ENJOYABLE TO READ AND AS TIMELY TO PRODUCE.*"

> **Plays by American Women**
> **Edited and with an introduction**
> **by Judith E. Barlow**

*"Barlow's introduction not only offers a description and analysis of the five playwrights but also sets them in an historical context."

—Booklist

A MAN'S WORLD
by Rachel Crothers
TRIFLES
by Susan Glaspell
MISS LULU BETT
by Zona Gale
PLUMES
by Georgia Douglas Johnson
MACHINAL
by Sophie Treadwell

These important dramatists did more than write significant new plays; they introduced to the American stage a new and vital character; the modern American woman in her quest for a forceful role in a changing American scene. It will be hard to remember that these women playwrights were ever forgotten.

APPLAUSE
THEATRE BOOK PUBLISHERS

1620